LEIGHTON FORD
A LIFE SURPRISED

LEIGHTON·FORD
A LIFE SURPRISED

NORMAN B. ROHRER

TYNDALE HOUSE
PUBLISHERS, INC. WHEATON, ILLINOIS

To those who have heard him preach
and have followed Jesus

PHOTO CREDITS: pg. 82—Åke Lundberg;
pg. 90—World Wide Pictures; pg. 120—Åke Lundberg;
pg. 138—A. J. Govinchuck; pg. 148—*Decision.*

All Bible quotations are from *The Living
Bible* unless otherwise noted.

Second printing, November 1981
Library of Congress Catalog Card Number 80-52764
ISBN 0-8423-2133-0, paper
Copyright © 1981 by Norman B. Rohrer and Leighton Ford
All rights reserved.
Printed in the United States of America

CONTENTS

A LIFE OBSERVED   7

THE SOURCE   13
[1] Twice Loved   15
     Dealing with adoption   21
[2] A House Divided   25
     How to cope with problem parents   29
[3] "This One Thing I Do"   35
     Accepting God's providences   41

THE CALL   45
[4] Blue Water   47
     Fighting loneliness and winning   51
[5] "Mr. President" at Fourteen   53

PREPARATION   59
[6] Wheaton   61
     Dealing with doubt   69
[7] Columbia   77
     There is a gift for you   83

LOVE, MARRIAGE, AND THE HOME   89
[8] Jean Coffey Graham   91
     In love: Are finders keepers?   97
[9] Hearthside—An Early Heaven   101
     What my children have taught me   113

THE WITNESS   119
[10] The Leighton Ford Crusades   121
     Failure can forecast success   135
[11] Just As They Are   139
[12] A Social Conscience   149
[13] Leighton and Billy   155
     'What is Billy like?'   163
     To my unknown parents   167

The Scottish theologian James Denney once suggested that the Church's theologians should be its evangelists and its evangelists should be its theologians.

Leighton Ford is both. If I were to step aside from my duties tomorrow I know of no one better qualified to take my place.

Leighton always is completely informed, always is current with his work, always has time to counsel a seeker, and always has time for his family. He has been more of a son to my mother than I have been—thoughtful, kind, loving, gracious. He is absolutely genuine, a man in whom there is no guile.

—Billy Graham

A LIFE OBSERVED

Leighton Frederick Sandys McCrea Ford was seventeen when his big gray Oldsmobile deposited him on the campus of Wheaton College in suburban Chicago one September day in 1949. He was alpine tall with large, clear blue eyes and was already a grade ahead of the rest of us campus newcomers.

Who was this conspicuous *Canadien* in tweed jackets, who scored higher in philosophy senior comprehensives than any other Wheatonite to date . . . who set a record for the number of preaching missions . . . and who won the hand of the campus prize, Jean Coffey Graham?

We assumed that "Leight" had been born entitled, springing from a nurturing family which had endowed him with the durable physical constitution, the emotional stability, the spiritual perception, and the mental acumen which he possessed to excess. The truth about his lineage was one of God's surprises.

I traveled with Leighton for two years on college-sponsored gospel teams, stood up with him when he married my classmate, and traded Christmas cards for a quarter of a century.

One of my earliest editorial assignments, beginning in

1958, was to write the weekly dispatches of the Evangelical Press News Service. In the flow of news bulletins from various agencies that poured into the office, I followed the rise of my buddy to positions of influence as an internationally known evangelist.

ITEM

Billy Graham lay ill with a constricted throat and the May 1961 opening of the Maine Road Stadium in Manchester, England, was at hand. Rain and cold winds buffeted the city. God's servant could only whisper. Should they cancel?

Walter Smyth placed an urgent transatlantic call. "Catch the next plane, Leighton," he said. "You've got to stand in for Bill."

Leighton, twenty-nine, stepped into a circle of floodlights, hardly able to see the 30,000 people in that yawning stadium as darkness deepened and rain continued to fall. When he had finished preaching that week, nearly a thousand Britishers had sloshed to the altar, their hearts warmed by hope and renewed by the Spirit.

In 1966 I was assigned to work in the press room of the World Congress on Evangelism in Berlin, and later to cover the 1969 U.S. Congress on Evangelism in Minnesota which was a spin-off of the international gathering three years earlier.

ITEM

On September 8, 1969, Leighton Ford keynoted the six-day Minneapolis congress with a message on "The Church and Evangelism in a Day of Revolution." American society was transforming itself into a series of subcultures, precipitated largely by civil injustices.

Leighton's words stung: "Why should the black man listen to us talk about a home in heaven, when we refuse to make him at home in our neighborhood and in our schools? What, I ask you, does this not *have to do with evangelism?"*

Time, Newsweek, *wire services and* The National Observer *heralded Leighton's speech as a sign of the emerging social conscience of evangelicals. Dr. Sherwood E. Wirt, editor emeritus of* Decision *magazine, and author of* The Social Conscience of the Evangelical, *called it "a turning point in bringing evangelical Christianity in the United States into a posture of social concern and responsibility."*

Later in that Congress Leighton had an opportunity to practice what he preached. A pair of hippies who had walked to the front of the auditorium and sat down were ushered out. The eviction angered the audience. Half an hour later Leighton came walking in with them amid applause and sat with them for the conclusion of a message by Keith Miller.

In 1970, Leighton phoned my office looking for scriptwriters to help produce a one-minute television commentary to be called, "The Leighton Ford TV Feature." These terse insights into the moods and attitudes of the times began following the evening news on forty-five television stations nationwide and are still an inspiring addendum to the often gloomy network fare.

ITEM
The bloodshot eye of the TV camera winked out and another feature was canned for release, but its message found acceptance before it left the studio. That evening a staff member at a related station phoned Leighton, "No one who will see you on TV is more needy than I. I've been unfaithful to my wife; my children don't trust me: I'm all alone. . . ."

The man had been led to Christ by a Charlotte pastor but his estranged wife was suspicious of his conversion. Leighton and Jean invited the estranged couple to their church. During a time together in Leighton's study afterward the wife listened carefully to her husband's appeal for forgiveness. Finally she turned to Leighton. "My husband has neglected me and the children so much I had decided to find a new husband who would care for us. And I have found him." She faced her spouse. "You are my 'new' husband."

Early in October 1975 the Fords' eldest son Sandy nearly died from a tachycardia associated with the Wolff-Parkinson-White syndrome (runaway heartbeat). One month after that near-fatal afternoon, appeals for prayer were dispatched as Sandy submitted to corrective surgery. Bill and Vonette Bright at Campus Crusade for Christ headquarters rose at 4 A.M. to pray; on the "700 Club," Pat Robertson called millions of listeners to a moment of prayer for the boy.

ITEM

As Sandy closed his eyes beneath the sterile sheets at Duke Medical Center in Durham, Leighton paced the dreary corridors. "Lord," he prayed, "you were Sandy's father before I was. He is your son before he is mine, in life or in death. . . ."

Surgeon Will C. Sealy exposed the organ through a median sternotomy and monitored the impulses of Sandy's heart. He cut the front circuit but the trouble wasn't there. He lifted the heart out and put his probe behind the heart . . . closer . . . closer . . . closer on the monitor of this medical team which had pioneered this procedure. He thrust his delicate rapier to within one millimeter of the normal conductor system. He cut and it was a success. Associates closed the wound and wired Sandy's rib cage shut. His strong heart beat normally again.

Through eyes wet with tears, Leighton read to Jean, Debbie, and Kevin, Hosea 6:1-3:

Come, let us return to the Lord; it is he who has torn us—he will heal us. He has wounded—he will bind us up. In . . . three [days] at the most, he will set us on our feet again, to live in his kindness! Oh, that we might know the Lord! Let us press on to know him, and he will respond to us as surely as the coming of dawn or the rain of early spring.

Being Billy Graham's brother-in-law has its special responsibilities and also its lighter side. Leighton has been introduced as Billy's mother-in-law, as his son-in-law, and once as his sister-in-law!

The grandest fun came unexpectedly from a distinguished pastor and educator who was presenting Leighton to students in a college chapel.

ITEM

"We are happy to have Leighton Ford as our speaker this morning," he began. "Perhaps some of you don't know that Leighton is married to Billy Graham's brother."

The crowd tittered and this venerable gentleman, nonplussed by the reaction, was so thrown off his usually impeccable stride that he concluded, "That makes Leighton Billy Graham's son-in-law."

Now the audience was beginning to double over with laughter. The speaker, startled and not realizing what he had said, plunged on to total disaster:

"So . . . now I present to you, Leighton Ford's brother-in-law, Billy Graham!"

The International Congress on World Evangelization had once again brought Leighton and me together, this time to the Palais de Beaulieu in Lausanne, Switzerland. Leighton worked behind the scenes as program chairman and I wrote daily news bulletins on what had transpired.

During those busy days I took a note to my old friend. An African clergyman was talking to him effusively. Leighton's face reflected tensions and pressures. He looked at me blankly, took my note, and then turned back to the African without saying a word. I heard no more from him.

Then suddenly our vacations overlapped at North Carolina's Grandfather Mountain and we supped with our wives in the dining room of a country club. Our conversation about the Divinity that had shaped our lives ranged far as we recounted the wonder of Godsends which transform the ordinary into the ordained.

Late that evening the format of this book emerged—a book dedicated not merely to the telling of one man's story but to the eulogizing of the great God of wonders who presses in upon us with divine surprise.

My journey back to Leighton's boyhood abode in "Canada the Good" triggered letters from his friends asking, "How much shall we tell him?"

"Tell him everything!" Leighton replied to each query.

Throughout the project he has been candid about his elusive roots, his compulsive obsession for perfection, his occasional preoccupation, his Canadian reserve, his bookish aloofness, his inability to lose without self-censure, his priesthood in the home, and his association with Billy Graham—mentor, brother-in-law, and for many years the surrogate father for his own perfunctory and hesitant adoptive dad.

The adventures of this life observed will enrich all who trust God for tomorrow because they have seen his fingerprint on today.

THE SOURCE

"I knew you before you were formed within your mother's womb; before you were born I sanctified you and appointed you as my spokesman to the world" (Jer. 1:5).

Leighton Ford as a young child.

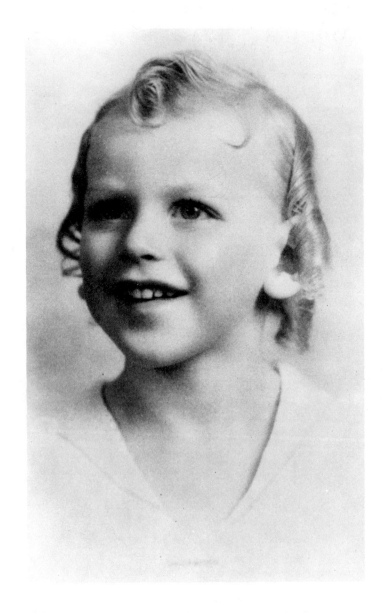

1

TWICE LOVED

The natives of Ontario who adopted Leighton Ford seemed coupled for the sake of strife. Charles Richard Ford, a watchmaker, had furtive blue eyes, a Santa Claus nose, puffed cheeks, and an apologetic stance; Etta Olive Shankland, a tiny woman reaching barely to five feet, was every inch a forthright, keen, and inventive person. She admired Queen Victoria but some considered her views about mutual characteristics exaggerated. Olive had even facial features ringed by a coiffure of tight curls. One remembers most vividly her curiously large, bright eyes. She was a paradox between a godly, polished, cultured woman and a bitter and paranoid wife.

Charles was content with conventional fare, Olive respected wealth and refinement; Charles attended church occasionally to be respectable, Olive committed her life and possessions to foreign missionary service in Africa. She never forgave Charlie for locating his jewelry store in the small agricultural and railroad center of 15,000 people called Chatham. She considered it too far west of the "Golden Horseshoe" of Ontario's industrial and cultural advantage, extending from Toronto around the west end of Lake Ontario. Olive was opinionated, somewhat condescending, demanding of her rights, and aloof from neighbors. Alternating moods found her warm, friendly, and earnest in her support of the work of God. She opened her home to a stream of foster daughters. Was she looking for a suitable person to train as a substitute for her forfeited missionary career?

"Ford's Jewellers" at 104 King Street West flourished in the roaring twenties. Charles borrowed heavily for inventory. He also siphoned off large portions of the profits to buy stock on margin. Olive warned him not to continue but he was ungovernable.

"You needn't worry, my Olivetta Shankaletta," he remonstrated. "Some day we'll be rich."

In 1927 fire destroyed his store. Two years later the stock market's "Black Monday" snatched away his budding fortune and piled up debts. Olive stepped in, made herself joint owner, and set up a schedule to pay creditors. Somehow they believed her when she promised that they would eventually get their money.

"You could learn more about finances from Olive Ford than from many a banker," a Toronto lawyer told me.

Charles scrimped so that Olive could lavish goods, services, and travel upon herself. He regularly arrived home well past midnight—first at their duplex, then at a three-story frame dwelling at Victoria and Gladstone, and finally at a large stucco house on Tecumseh Park at Stanley and Williams Streets.

One summer night Charles locked up the store, ambled down King Street, crossed the footbridge to the park, and walked the several blocks to their house beneath the towering shade trees. When he opened the door Olive was waiting for him in an angry mood. "I'm going shopping in the morning and I need more money," she demanded.

"Well, I *gave* you money this afternoon," Charles replied. "No more."

"The safe is full of money. I'll go to the store in the morning and get what I need."

"That money is for inventory. Leave it alone."

Charles went upstairs and slammed his bedroom door, but Olive wasn't finished. She continued her harangue in the hallway so he went into the bathroom and flushed the toilet repeatedly to drown her outbursts with noise. Olive refused to go to bed so Charles dressed, left the house, and stayed away all night, as he was to do often in the future. It was the start of a lifetime of quarreling which led eventually to their separation.

Olive's retreats into paranoia grew more frequent. "Home" for Charles became his watchmaker's bench, "romance" the sport of lawn bowling which he mastered, "companionship" the wine bottle hidden in his gem cabinet.

When emotionally stable, Olive remembered her vows to the Lord. She was a stalwart supporter of First Presbyterian Church. The age of thirty-five approached. Would the Lord yet give her a child? This request was on her tongue often, but she may have begun to doubt that her longing would ever be fulfilled.

On October 22, 1931, the lights of New York City were dimmed in honor of inventor Thomas A. Edison who had been buried at the age of eighty-four. But on that date a new life was added to the family of man—one who would have a profound influence on the life of Charles and Olive Ford and millions more.

Mother love stabbed a young mother's heart as she studied the profile of her new son in the sterile bed at Toronto General Hospital. She memorized each little contour of his baby face. Yes, she would remember this child always—beyond this tryst so agonizingly brief.

She touched a slim finger to his aristocratic nose and smiled as he wrinkled his brow and emitted a shallow, staccato cry. The sound of a nurse's voice echoed in the cream-colored corridor outside. "Doctor, here are the papers for the new little fellow."

The young mother held her son tightly. Although tears stung her eyes she was calm as she studied the white band on his tiny wrist: Toronto General Hospital, October 22, 1931. Number. . . .

"Get him into the nursery and feed him," a doctor's voice interrupted somewhere down the hall.

"Won't his mother want to do that?"

"Look, the sooner we take over, the better it will be for

everyone. Apparently the baby's going to be adopted. Let's make it as easy as possible for them. The family's high-born on both sides—very religious, too."

A squeaky cart wobbled past the door and the young mother grew tense. Her baby yawned peacefully. The nurse appeared, smiling. "Miss . . ."

"Yes, I overheard."

The nurse cradled the baby in her arms and was gone. The mother did not venture beyond her room but she loosed her imagination to wander along the corridor, glancing into the glass-enclosed nursery to single out one child—her son.

Hours became days and she was released, returning to a college campus. She did not hear the nurse call the doctor and report: "I have a message from the front desk. A Mrs. Charles Ford and her lawyer are here to receive the baby. . . ."

. . . The southbound Canadian Pacific Limited sent its lonely whistle across the barren autumn plains of Kent County, dived with a roar under the highway trestles, and then burst into steam.

"Chatham!" the conductor called. "Chatham, next stop."

Only a high school girl who was working for the Fords was told the names of the baby's natural parents. Mrs. Ford wanted at least one outsider to know, fearing that her adopted son might in later years fall in love with a sister and bear abnormal children.

She named him "Leighton," conceivably after Canada's Envoy Extraordinary and Minister Plenipotentiary at Washington, D.C. . . . "Frederick" for her uncle who was killed at Vimy Ridge, France, during World War I before he could complete his ministerial studies at Wycliffe College . . . and "Sandys" in honor of Mrs. Lucy Sandys, an Anglican deaconess. Later Olive added the name "McCrea," a name which a close family friend thinks exposes a clue to Leighton's Irish or Scottish lineage.

Olive sang hymns to her baby and folded his tiny hands for prayer. She commissioned a carpenter to build a walnut prayer bench which stood like an altar in an alcove outside her son's room. Each morning as Leighton grew he would kneel under Olive's watchful eye on the crimson cushion and rest his folded hands on the upright bar to talk with a loving heavenly Father. Olive was determined to make her home a nursery for the Almighty.

Her actions seemed to be an attempt to fulfill her own frustrated missionary career by imposing her will on her son. She had been unable to rule Charles; in subtle ways she was setting herself up as Leighton's alter ego.

A child's view of himself is determined largely by what he thinks is his parents' view of him. In early boyhood Leighton might have imagined that he was the cause of his parents' anxieties. Children tend to blame themselves for their parents' feelings and avoid acting in ways that make their parents anxious. They strive for acceptance by being "perfect." The result is a perfectionism that continually compares them with the idealized "me."

It would have been natural for Leighton to try to control his parents' anger by being obedient. He accepted his mother's spiritual force-feeding and today is thankful for it. Another child might have had his love for God extinguished. The thought of rebelling didn't occur to Leighton. He sees the hand of God in placing him in that strict home. The pain of never knowing his natural parents is keen, but there are redeeming factors, as he explains in the following commentary on his childhood.

1936: Leighton and his mother, Etta Olive Shankland Ford, on the beach.

DEALING WITH ADOPTION

When I was about twelve years old, my mother told me that I was adopted. I think she handled it wisely. Until then I had never suspected that I was adopted. I should have, because my mother was barely five feet tall and my father was only about five feet six! Both of them were rather stout. I was already growing into a tall, lanky youth who would end up being six feet four.

I didn't suspect anything until that cool autumn day in Toronto when my mother and I went for a walk in High Park near the apartment where her two aunts lived and where we were probably visiting at the time. Mother intimated that there had been an "accident" of some sort with my natural parents. At that time I supposed that they had been killed in an accident. Looking back I imagine that I was the "accident"! Mother stressed that she and my father chose to have me because they wanted a child of their own.

From that moment on, being adopted always gave to me a sense of being "special," not in the sense of being better than anybody else but in the sense of being really loved, really chosen, and really wanted. There was an emotional security in this.

Later on I read the Apostle Paul's words in Romans 8:15 that the believer is "adopted into the bosom of his [God's] family" which enables us to say to God, "Father, Father." The Holy Spirit witnesses with us that we are the children of God and therefore we are heirs of all that God has along with Christ (Rom. 8:16, 17). Paul also taught in Galatians 4:4, 5 that God sent his Son so that "he could adopt us as his very own sons." He wrote to the Ephesians that God's "unchanging plan has always been to adopt us into his own family by sending Jesus Christ to die for us. And he did this because he wanted to!" (Eph. 1:5).

I believe that God in his providence led my parents to choose and adopt me. What would have happened if I had been brought up instead by my natural parents? That's totally a mystery, but I do know that in my adopted family I was exposed at the earliest age to the Bible, to prayer, and to influences which would lead me not only to know God but to serve him. And what was true of me, I believe, is true of all of us whether we are adopted or not.

God knows our lives—where we are going to be born and who our parents are going to be. He superintends every detail to bring us to the place where we might know him as our Father. God does not want any of us to be lonely orphans in this world. Through Jesus Christ and completely by his grace he wants to take us who are slaves to sin and separated from him and adopt us into his family so that we might have all the family rights for time and eternity.

It used to be that I didn't mention very often that I was adopted. In more recent years I frequently tell people when I am preaching that I am adopted. Often when I do this some adopted child or adoptive parents will come up and say how much that meant. Some are upset about being adopted. I remember a girl in her early teens in Pennsylvania who said she felt "terrible." I hope I was able to help her feel "special," as I do.

A man from Greece who had immigrated to Melbourne, Australia, attended one of our meetings there and heard me mention my adoption. It rang home to him because he had been, too. The message I brought about Jesus Christ began to make more sense to him, he said, and he accepted Christ that night.

Until I was in my forties and my adopted parents had both died, I didn't think a lot about my natural parents. But in more recent years I launched a search to find out all I could about them. My quest did not go unrewarded, as I shall explain in a later chapter. Perhaps it was because I had read Roots, *and articles on adopted children who had found their natural parents. Or perhaps it was just these mid-years of my life when I think we are all looking more intently for roots. But in any case, I have been trying to find out everything I can. I wanted to know* who my natural parents are, to find out if I have any half brothers or sisters living, to know something about my heritage, and especially to share with them what Jesus Christ has come to mean as the center of my life.

All of us have the need to belong. Ultimately, that need is for more than natural or adopted parents. It is a need to be able to say to God, "My Father," I have read some place that Anna Marx, the daughter of Karl Marx, the father of communism, told a friend that she had come across an old prayer which began, "Our Father, who art in heaven." With her secular upbringing she did not recognize the Lord's Prayer but she told her friend wistfully, "If there really was a God like the one described in that prayer, I could believe in him."

As an adopted son of the heavenly Father I would like to say, "Anna, he is real. He is a home for all your longings. Believe in him."

Being adopted by God brings great privileges but also great responsibility. He has chosen us to bear "the family likeness" (Rom. 8:29). He expects us not to dishonor the family name, but to live a life worthy of being God's child.

John puts the privilege and responsibility into perspective: "See how very much our heavenly Father loves us, for he allows us to be called his children—think of it—and we really are! But since most people don't know God, naturally they don't understand that we are his children. Yes, dear friends, we are already God's children, right now, and we can't even imagine what it is going to be like later on. But we do know this, that when he comes we will be like him, as a result of seeing him as he really is. And everyone who really believes this will try to stay pure because Christ is pure" (1 John 3:1-3).

Leighton Ford as a boy.

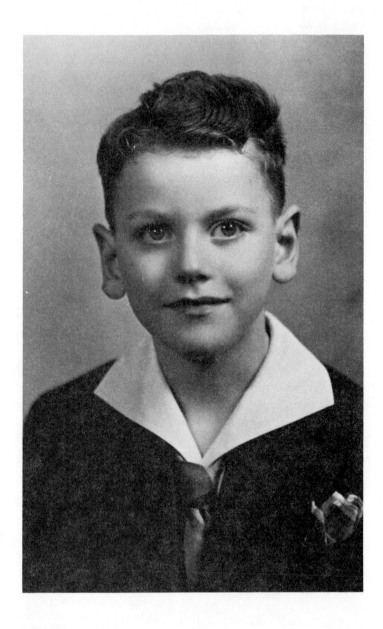

2

A HOUSE DIVIDED

Olive believed that spiritual attainment was not on the side of the fainthearted. Raised as an Anglican, she respected the sovereignty of God but she linked her own hand with Providence to expose her son to the best evangelical influences.

Olive was not surprised when Henry Frost, a director of the China Inland Mission, cradled her baby in his arms, prayed, and announced: "Mrs. Ford, I believe God has given you this child for a purpose." Leighton was reminded of that 1933 episode repeatedly.

She was not surprised either when she saw her son at the age of three call his chums to a funeral for a dead robin he had discovered in the backyard. They had to sit in a circle and be very still while Leighton preached a "sermon" over the deceased.

At four, Leighton collected his coins and had his mother send them as a tithe to *The Evangelical Christian* magazine in Toronto to purchase missionary gift subscriptions. The editors featured Leighton in a back-page subscription appeal titled, "There is a lad here. . . ."

The overprotective mother must have been pleased one Sunday morning when her son in knee pants walked up to a stranger at church and said, "I'm the minister's number one boy."

As a toddler Leighton began his annual summer treks with his mother to Bible conferences at Canadian Keswick in the north of Ontario. On the interminable train rides Olive coached him as he memorized the entire seventeenth chapter of St. John's Gospel and other selected verses. At Keswick he climbed rocks, learned to row, and swam in frigid Lake Rosseau. Mostly he attended Bible meetings. Before he was twelve he would be writing brief sermons and showing them to the old men of Keswick who labeled them "Quite good!" At Keswick Leighton made his commitment to Christ at the age of five in a children's meeting conducted by Frances Thomas.

The day of Leighton's conversion in 1936 is vividly recalled. A breeze off Lake Rosseau tugged at the skirts and snapped the shirts of the children as they filed into a house at Canadian Keswick for Frances Thomas' daily "Happy Hour." Five-year-old Leighton, a bit taller and thinner than most, took his place on the front row.

Amid her flannelgraph, chalkboard, and colorful teaching accoutrements the former missionary to China held the youngsters spellbound with the story of Nicodemus, that distinguished Jewish teacher who once asked Jesus, "How can a man be born when he is old?" And then, as she did after each meeting at Keswick, Miss Thomas asked the children to raise their hands if they wanted to respond to God's invitation for salvation. Leighton's hand shot up.

"No, Leighton," Miss Thomas whispered. "You're too young. Please be still."

Again she gave the invitation and again Leighton raised his hand. She tried once more to dissuade him.

The third time Leighton's hand was raised Miss Thomas perceived that the boy of five had understood and was prepared to make a commitment to the Savior.

The economic depression was loosening its grip in 1936, but how to spend the increased profits from Ford's Jewellers remained a constant irritation between the co-owners of the store. On the one hand Leighton was indulged completely; on the other hand he was held accountable to his mother for every hour spent, and every order carried out. He cannot remember any request denied, except for a second volume of the *Big Chum* series

Mrs. Ford wouldn't buy him in Toronto on a shopping spree. One volume would have to do. A street photographer snapped a picture shortly afterward but Leighton refused to smile, pouting like Puddleglum about his denied request.

At six, in 1937, a lifelong interest in piano was awakened with lessons by Whitney Scherer on the Fords' big Heintzman. Leighton needed no prodding to practice but when he had to be punished for disobedience in other areas Mrs. Ford never spanked; she lectured. She could sustain her spiel for hours, gushing on relentlessly until Leighton had to put his mind elsewhere to keep from going crazy. Was this early conditioning for later mental preoccupation?

That year Nora O'Neill, a spunky Irish Catholic girl from rural Kent Bridge, Ontario, applied to work in the Ford home while she attended the Chatham Collegiate Institute (high school). After Nora's interview six-year-old Leighton shook his blond curls. "How old is she anyway?" he asked cautiously.

"Fifteen," Mrs. Ford replied. "Why?"

Knowing that Nora would probably be giving him his bath, he decided, "She doesn't look old enough to me."

"She *must* be old enough," his mother explained, "because they call her 'Miss O'Neill.' "

"I can't help it," Leighton insisted. "She doesn't look old enough to me."

While Leighton was in the early elementary grades Mrs. Ford took in yet another foster daughter. Alden Morrison was closer to being a sister than anyone in the flux. The evening she arrived Leighton sent a message from his bedroom: "Mum, go downstairs and tell Aldy I have a friend who makes my black heart white."

Alden lived her entire youth in the shadow of the adopted son. She was slow and deliberate, Leighton was quick and perceptive; Alden seldom spoke, Leighton was loquacious and assertive; Aldy was short while Leighton grew tall and wiry. Her slow pace displeased Mrs. Ford, but she kept Alden until 1948, when she was suddenly sent away. Alden settled in Ingersoll, Ontario, where she became the wife of factory worker Mel Carter, now deceased.

"I felt sorry for Aldy," a friend of the family's commented. "She was definitely a second-class citizen in that home."

Alden alienated herself further from Olive by taking the side of Charles in family tiffs. The nocturnal fighting gradually became more frequent. Often Leighton was jolted awake by the violent quarreling of his parents— Olive demanding money or information, Charles barricading himself in the bathroom where his sequential flushings drowned out the angry screams of his frantic wife. The boy never knew in the morning whether his father had stayed the night or fled to a hotel.

To the end of her life Olive imagined that sinister men in black cars were following her, monitoring her movements, surrounding her small house in Ottawa where she spent her final years alone. Later she resented Leighton's marriage and turned up unannounced to disrupt his life at inconvenient seasons. Olive made it difficult for Charles to embrace Christianity which, to his way of thinking, had fueled the alienation between them.

HOW TO COPE WITH PROBLEM PARENTS

It has become popular to blame hang-ups on parents. But Charlie Brown in "Peanuts" gave a mortal blow to these pseudo-psychologies. He had gone to Lucy, his amateur psychiatrist, for some counseling and she had told him that his problem was with his parents. "But Lucy," protested Charlie, "didn't you ever think about the fact that parents had parents?"

Nevertheless, because God the Father has placed us in families, our relationships with our parents and how we handle them do affect us for good or for ill.

IMPERFECT PARENTS

All children have imperfect parents just as parents have imperfect children. But the Bible, which is realistic about our human frailties and sins, nevertheless tells children to honor and obey their parents. Paul writes to Christian children, "Children, obey your parents; this is the right thing to do because God has placed them in authority over you. Honor your father and mother. This is the first of God's Ten Commandments that ends with a promise. And this is the promise: that if you honor your father and mother, yours will be a long life, full of blessing" (Eph. 6:1-3).

When Paul says to obey parents "because God has placed them in authority over you," he is not necessarily suggesting a situation where parental orders might be contrary to the Lord's will. More likely he is thinking of the basis of relationships in the Christian home. Through the grace of Christ we have an even more compelling motive than the law of the Old Testament for honoring our parents. Paul points out that we should obey because it is right, and it is wise. For God promises that we will be blessed in obeying. Rebelling against parents is one of those marks of general disobedience which will characterize the "last days" (Matt. 10:21). The civilization which has lost its reverence for parents is in trouble.

How long must a child obey? Always, no matter what the situation? Not so, in my judgment. Looking back, I am deeply thankful for my mother. She taught me to honor the Lord, to pray, to read the Bible, to serve Christ. She encouraged me in the ministry. She loved me and comforted me and affirmed me and gave me every opportunity to develop my gifts. She held up high ideals and goals.

Yet as I entered my late teens and she grew older, she became mentally ill. She had always been strong-willed and now she became even more domineering. In her illness she began to live under strange and fantastic delusions of persecution and to make irrational and unreasonable demands. When I went off to my first year of college, she also rented an apartment in Wheaton and spent some months there. Her life was so much wrapped up in mine that she found it impossible to let me go. When Jeanie and I planned to be married, I was halfway through seminary and Jeanie was already employed, but my mother frantically opposed the idea of our being married. If I had done exactly what she wanted, would this have been God's will? I doubt it. Rather I probably would never have been married.

There comes a point when parents need to let go, and when children need to take responsibility under God for their own lives. Certainly Christian children are always to honor their parents, and to obey them up until that point when they become adults. Just when that point occurs may not be clear cut. It certainly comes when a young man "leaves his mother and father and cleaves to his wife."

For single people the "leaving" point might not be as clear. There may be anguish of conscience. Parents should be wise enough to know when to let go. If not, then children at some point, seeking wise counsel from others, will need to take a stand with a sense of honor. This is never an easy separation.

Scars were left from the later years of my relationship with my mother, and in some ways I wish that I could relive them.

There were some turbulent times when I felt deep anger and was adamant. I wish I had better understood myself and her. But unless children have some breathing space to become responsible persons in the Lord they cannot grow to maturity as they should.

UNCONVERTED PARENTS

One of the questions I am asked most frequently is how young people who have become Christians should witness to parents who are unbelievers. Peter's advice to Christian wives of non-Christian husbands was to live so that "they will be won by your respected, pure behavior. Your godly lives will speak to them better than any words" (1 Pet. 3:1).

That can also apply to children witnessing to their parents. Young converts in the enthusiasm and zeal of their newfound faith, may come on too strong. They return home from their experiences on the campus or at summer camp determined to win over their parents, but their zeal may produce the opposite effect. In the same way a husband's masculine pride makes him defensive when he feels that his wife is out to change him, so parents who through the years have tried to teach and train their children may well react negatively when children whose tears they have wiped and bottoms they have spanked start pronouncing "the truth." And if they are not familiar with basic Christianity they may be afraid that their children are caught up in some bizarre cult.

My advice to young people is to go slowly. Tell your parents about the experience you have had. Explain to them what you have come to believe about Jesus Christ, if they are open to it. But don't push beyond what they are ready to receive. And most of all, pray that your attitude and life style may be such that they may be impressed by it and see the change in you.

Some of the young people in a Bible study in our city had non-Christian parents. On Saturdays they made a practice of going into one of their homes and volunteering to wash windows, mop the kitchen floor, and generally clean up and be helpful. A cookout to which they invited their parents gave an opportunity to explain the motive behind their actions.

My own father, so far as I know, was not a believer until late in his life. As a boy he was a nominal church attender but as I was growing up I never knew him to pray or read the Bible or talk about God or Christ. Only seldom did he go to church with us. My mother, being as determined and aggressive as she was about her faith, probably turned him off to some extent.

Several times in my late teens I tried to talk to him about his relationship with the Lord but he and I both found that very difficult. As the years went by his love for me and his interest in the work that God had given to me opened him up. I will never forget the night at Miami Beach when he raised his hand after I had preached, in answer to my appeal for those who wished to commit their lives to Christ. He never became what I would describe as a strong Christian but at least the seed of faith was there. Out of this experience I would encourage a quiet, patient, prayerful, loving witness—sharing the word of the gospel when there is opportunity, and letting Christ live his life through us. This approach, I believe, will eventually bear fruit.

AGING PARENTS
People in the middle years of life have a double responsibility—for their school-age children on one hand and their aging parents on the other. This can be a tough squeeze. It's difficult to work out priorities and responsibilities with love and grace.

Our culture tends to put more stock in youth than in age. But one of the prime marks of our Christianity is the way we treat our parents when they need our support and love. Paul told Timothy, "But if they have children or grandchildren, they are the ones who should take the responsibility, for kindness should begin at home, supporting needy parents. This is something that pleases God very much" (1 Tim. 5:4).

Putting this principle into practice is not always easy. When our parents have to leave their own home, should we take them into ours or place them in a retirement home? How often and when should we visit? Circumstances and personalities are different. There are no blanket answers. But surely we can seek to treat our parents with the same kind of love and firmness (espe-

cially when some of them become a bit childish) as we wanted them to treat us when we were wholly dependent upon them.

My mother-in-law, Mrs. Frank Graham, has been a great blessing to me. Since my parents died she has become more like a mother. My wife and I, and she and her other children, have wrestled with the question of care for her. At one time she left her beautiful farm home for a condominium but she was so miserable that we had to arrange for her to move back where she would have her own place and her flowers and her birds and her dog—and now her goat as well!

Trying to help her decide whether to stay where she has her own things or whether to go to the security of a retirement home has demanded many hours of time, love, thought, and prayer. The answers still aren't easy. But she has more than repaid whatever little time we have invested by the example of her faith and wisdom that has grown more graceful with age.

A Youth for Christ rally in Chatham, Ontario. Second from the right is Chatham's YFC director, Leighton Ford, age fourteen.

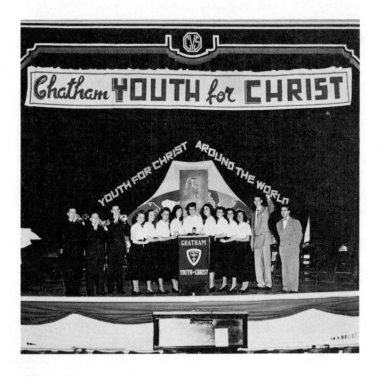

3

"THIS ONE THING I DO"

At thirteen Leighton stood nearly six feet tall, wore size twelve shoes, and weighed little more than a hundred pounds. He took top academic scores at McKeough School, read armloads of adventure books and tasted, chewed, and digested the biographies of such stalwart evangelists as R. A. Torrey, James Gilmore, David Livingstone, Charles G. Finney, and Dwight L. Moody.

Once when Pastor and Mrs. Marcus Scott Fulton were visiting the Ford home, Leighton rushed in from school almost out of breath, skidded on the floor, dropped his books on the table, and tried to make a quick exit. "Leighton! Leighton!" his mother called, "Doctor and Mrs. Fulton are here."

Leighton retraced his steps with chagrin on his face but with a twinkle in his large blue eyes. During the visit Mrs. Ford reminded Leighton, "The world needs another Moody."

"I know, mother," Leighton shot back, "but I want to go out and play ball."

Dr. Fulton visited with the boy for a few minutes then helped him make his escape to the ball field.

Leighton learned to love every sport. Fond recollections stir when he remembers sitting in front of the big cabinet radio with his father on Saturday nights to hear Foster Hewett announce in the Maple Leaf Gardens of Toronto: "Good evening, hockey fans, it's hockey night in Canada." Leighton was usually named goalie at neighborhood hockey games because he was the only kid with a set of pads. Within the confines of game rules Leighton could play as furiously as Jehu drove his chariot and was never satisfied with coming in second.

A friendly kid named Danny Goldsmith occasionally, then regularly, tagged along home after school to trade commemorative stamps. Leighton liked to have a companion because he could never be sure his mother would be there to greet him or whether she was in another city fleeing imagined pursuers. Many times he gave Danny precious commemorative stamps, not wanting anything in trade. Material things were expendable to Leighton. Most things were replaceable simply by a request.

Leighton and Danny rattled around Chatham after permission was arranged with Mrs. Ford. Often they would wander to Detroit by train for the big Voice of Christian Youth rallies or to Toronto to take in special appearances of Charles E. Fuller and the "Old Fashioned Revival Hour" singers, the meetings of former evangelist Chuck Templeton, or the missionary conferences of Oswald J. Smith. To get money the boys would amble into Ford's Jewellers. "Dad, Danny and I would like to go to Detroit this Saturday." Charles would reach for his wallet then ask where they planned to stay and on what train they would return. Then he would dole out thirty . . . forty . . . even fifty dollars. Leighton once took a large wad of fifty-dollar bills from his father's safe so he and Danny could play touch football in the store. He enjoyed throwing coins out of the window of a hotel to see if he could hit the people below. Danny recalls that his aim was poor and "he always missed."

Once in Toronto with Danny, Leighton asked a waitress, "What's this 'Beans and Wieners'?" At home he was never served such plain food. While his chum ordered special big city cooking, Leighton had his first taste of beans and wieners.

Even before Leighton had his driver's license there was a new car in the garage which neither parent could drive. He and Danny liked to back it out to the street and then cruise into the garage. The sport lasted until Aldy tried it and crashed through the back of the garage. Later Leighton decorated the Oldsmobile as a "float" for his youth rally in the annual Chatham Christmas Parade and arranged for Jean Cornelius to drive it.

By 1944 the Fords' facade of respectability had worn thin. While his parents scandalized the neighborhood with their fighting, Leighton tried to keep himself aloof, driving to excel . . . studying for top grades . . . writing sermons . . . winning at sports.

In Detroit one day he and Danny happened upon a street-side "Voice-O-Graph" booth. Leighton put fifty cents into it and cut a one-minute recording of the song "On the Jericho Road." He sang both the melody and the extra bass parts, just like the Old Fashioned Revival Hour Quartet. He also narrated an imaginary baseball game featuring Hank Greenberg and the Pirates and ending the phonograph abruptly with a crisp appeal: "Believe on the Lord Jesus Christ and thou shalt be saved." On a second phonograph he did a clever and believable impersonation of a hockey broadcaster, narrating with machine-gun speed an imaginary game featuring such names as O'Conner and Richard over the "Imperial Oil Broadcast."

The family's facade collapsed on Monday morning, Christmas Day, 1944. Leighton slipped into his green-and-brown robe and descended the stairs of their house on Tecumseh Park. The early sunlight lay in pools on the living room floor beneath the Christmas tree and he smelled bacon frying.

"Mother, you're up!" he exclaimed, wondering at the unusual sight of Olive preparing breakfast.

"It's going to be a special day," she replied.

"Special?" Leighton asked, slipping into his chair at the table.

"Yes, dad's going to church with us. Afterward he's taking us to The Capital."

"What's playing?"

"The movie is *Leave Her to Heaven*," Mrs. Ford explained as Charles and Alden joined them in the kitchen.

"I'm glad we can all go," Leighton said.

After breakfast Mr. Ford called a taxi and soon they were seated snugly in a pew at the historic, ornate red-brick sanctuary of First Presbyterian Church at Wellington and Fifth Streets, listening to Dr. Marcus Scott Fulton expound the Scriptures from the Reformed point of view. The Ford family walked to The Capital downtown for the featured show afterward and thence to the jewelry store en route home to pick up an item. Olive asked her husband for money.

"There's not that much left," Charles replied.

"There would be enough money if you hadn't thrown it away as you did on those worthless stocks," she pouted.

"For God's sake, Olive, will you stop bringing that up? It happened twenty years ago. Forget it!"

"How can I forget it? It would have made us rich."

Charles grew quiet but Olive continued to raise her voice. Leighton went to the store's balcony lounge to read, wishing she would stop. For half an hour Olive needled and badgered her husband. Somehow the shouting started and then came a shove . . . and finally angry tirades that knocked a box of crystals to the floor and shook the glass counter displays.

Olive ran to the large floor safe under the balcony, screaming uncontrollably in mental anguish as she clung to the top of the safe. Charles' face paled and he tried to pull her back from the safe which she was kicking insanely. Leighton wanted to hide, but he ran to his mother and tried to hold her until she stopped thrashing and was restored to her senses. Alden remained out of sight, joining them when the storm had subsided and they were all ready to lock the door, proceed respectably down King Street, cross the bridge to the park, and walk into the safe retreat of their house.

Life was never again as calm or innocent for Leighton.

He realized now that his mother had more than an occasional mental digression. She began taking more unexplained trips because she believed communists were after her . . . that Charles was one of them . . . that black cars were monitoring her movements . . . and that her husband was trying to get her into an asylum and cut her out of the business. And then the nightmare would pass temporarily and she would be back in the store waiting on customers and running her home.

After that black Monday Leighton understood better the sufferings his father had quietly endured. He understood why in recent years he had worked until three every morning at his bench and why he had to barricade himself in his bedroom to escape the furious accusations of the woman he had asked to marry him a quarter of a century earlier.

Somewhere among Leighton's books were the lines of Pope in *Essay on Man*:

"Laugh where we must, be candid where we can,
But vindicate the ways of God to man."

1949: Leighton Ford introduces his friend Danny Goldsmith to Billy Graham during Billy's first visit to Chatham.

ACCEPTING GOD'S PROVIDENCES

Once I saw a poster that said, "To believe in God is to know that life will be full of surprise after surprise, and every one good." At one point I would have thought that unrealistically saccharine. Now I have come to believe that poster expresses the heart of Christian faith—an affirmation of God's providence and master control in the universe and in our lives.

The lady who helped lead me to Christ as a child used to sign her letters, "Frances Thomas, Rom. 8:28." As a boy I thought that was actually a part of her title or her name! Only later did I learn that "Rom. 8:28" stood for Paul's letter to the Romans, chapter 8, verse 28, which expresses a great confidence, "And we know that in all things God works for the good of those who love him, who have been called according to his purpose" (NIV). Miss Thomas' life exemplified this truth. She had little of this world's goods. She often lived not knowing where money for her next meal would come from. She was a large woman and suffered ill health, but I can still remember her sweet and trusting smile, and her belief that in all things God was working together for her good.

This verse teaches more than the power of positive thinking. It tells us of the love and power and wisdom of a sovereign God. These words do not express a naive, Pollyannaish optimism about life. The eighth chapter of Romans speaks of suffering, persecution, trials, hardships, and even death. But in all of this, Paul rises to the triumphant affirmation that in all these things we are more than conquerors because nothing can separate us from the love of God which is in Jesus Christ our Lord.

To be a Christian is to affirm God's control. From the beginning to the end of my life he has a purpose. His eyes didn't widen in surprise when I was born! With perfect wisdom and timing, God allows to come into my life those things which will be his tools to accomplish his purpose in my life. Of course not everything that happens is good in itself. Some of life's happenings taken merely on their own terms are deeply hurtful. Yet in the larger, total perspective of God's master plan we believe that "in all things God works for the good of those who love him." As someone has said, "God's love wills what is best for me. God's wisdom knows what is best for me. God's power achieves what is best for me."

To believe in God's providence is to believe that absolutely nothing can come into my life unless God allows it and that God can use it for his purpose. God works in everything "for good" but what is "good"? The "good" Paul speaks of here doesn't simply mean my happiness or my comfort; rather, Paul goes on to say that "From the very beginning God decided that those who came to him—and all along he knew who would—should become like his Son, so that his Son would be the First, with many brothers" (Rom. 8:29).

As I reflect on my own life I can see many of God's surprises. Why should I have been born at the moment that I was, and available for adoption to the parents who chose me? Wounds came because of the conflicts my parents had and the illness my mother went through, and some of these scars have stayed with me and caused turmoil in my life. But I also know that if I had not been taken into the home of my parents I might not have been exposed to Christian teaching and influence, taken to the Canadian Keswick Conference where I was taught the Scriptures, been involved in Youth for Christ through which I met Billy Graham, and finally been called into the ministry. If I had not met Billy Graham at the time I did I probably would not have gone to Wheaton College, nor would I have met his sister who became my wife, whose loving, strong, stable support has been exactly what God knew I needed. Later on when our son Sandy faced a severe heart problem and serious surgery I could see, looking back, how God allowed it to come into our lives at just the right time. Through Sandy's illness we learned to depend more on the sovereignty of God, to value prayer, to express our own needs and fears more openly to other people and to become more vulnerable, more human, and hopefully more reflective of Christ.

Sometimes I am asked what I believe to be the secret of a happy, victorious Christian life. I have come to see that there is no one formula or magic way of achieving success or growth. The only secret is to believe that, sometimes mysteriously, but always lovingly, God is working out in his time what is best through respondent faith and trust.

Brother Lawrence expressed this in a way I like very much. Brother Lawrence was a cook in a monastery in medieval times, and the man who originated the phrase, "practicing the presence of God." Early in his life Brother Lawrence strove to win God's favor through strict self-denial and religious discipline. Yet he was never able to achieve a sense of God's favor and acceptance. One late winter afternoon he was sitting outside under a tree, and as he looked at that tree he began to ponder the mysterious secret of growth. He realized that it was not time for leaves and blossoms to be on that tree. As soon as spring would come, and with it the sun, then would come blossoms and leaves and the fruit.

"I was like the tree in winter," he said. "Myself, I was nothing—dead, barren, without fruit. Like the tree I couldn't change by struggling or sheer effort. I, too, must wait for the hand of my Maker to touch me with life, and change my winter of barren unfruitfulness—in his own time—into first the spring of new life and then the summer and the fall of flower and fruit.

"Suddenly I saw what 'providence' was all about—it is simply believing that God has the power in the world to do all things well for us, if we will only submit to his loving, patient rule. Nothing we can do—beyond trusting him—will speed up his will or make things happen which he is not ready to do in us.

"At that moment, sitting there in the grass, my acts of worship, my attempts at discipline—all the effort I had put into trying to please God—was swallowed up in an enormous sense of love for him. The One who patiently led the trees and the plants

*through their seasons would also lead me if I would only submit to his loving and powerful hand."**

With Brother Lawrence I would define this as a Christian's attitude to life—not to shake our fist in God's face with stubborn rebellion and say, "Thy will be hanged," nor to fold our hands in pious resignation and sigh, "Thy will be endured," but rather to affirm with joyous confidence, trust, and cooperation, "Thy will be done!"

Closer Than a Brother, by David Winter, (Harold Shaw Publishers), pp. 19, 20.

THE CALL

"Don't let anyone think little of you because you are young. . . . Be a pattern for them in your love, your faith, and your clean thoughts" (1 Tim. 4:12).

The "Pee Wee Quartet" sings at a Chatham Youth for Christ rally, directed by Leighton Ford (second from left in the front row).

4

BLUE WATER

The year 1945 launched three historic movements that would alter the course of Leighton's life. In Brantford, one hundred miles northeast of Chatham, an inter-church youth evangelistic thrust called Canadian Youth Fellowship was formed by Evon Hedley; in Chicago, a youthful preacher named Torrey Johnson and auto mechanic Bob Cook founded a movement called "Youth For Christ"; in Chatham, a public accountant named Roy Martin opened the Blue Water Bible Conference twenty miles north of the city.

All three of these agencies were points of a kaleidoscope which, as they turned on the wheel of Providence, became a beautiful pattern of opportunity and influence in the life of teenager Leighton Ford.

At this point in his pilgrimage Leighton was persuaded to attend Blue Water's very first youth conference. It was attended largely by young people from the Christian and Missionary Alliance Church in nearby Windsor, Ontario. Leighton observed that these peers were alive, eager, and full of joy as they sang gospel choruses—not like the reserved youth at his more formal church. They seemed happier than any kids Leighton had ever seen in his Christian life. He wondered why.

Oswald J. Smith, pastor of People's Church in Toronto, came to address the conference. As the fidgety minister began his message titled, "The Morning Watch," Leighton let his mind wander to the ball field. The lure of the game was more attractive that bright morning than the prospect of sitting through a sermon.

"I am a nervous individual by nature," the speaker was saying. Leighton had noticed that.

"When I pray, I don't kneel down . . . I don't sit . . . and I don't stand."

What does he do, fly? Leighton wondered.

"In order to keep my mind alert when I pray I walk up and down. . . ."

The idea fascinated Leighton. To him, prayer was kneeling at the altar upstairs in his house, or repeating memorized lines at meal time.

"And I pray aloud," Dr. Smith continued, "to keep my mind from wandering and to keep from repeating the same words over and over. Sometimes I take the words of a Psalm and make them my prayer. . . ."

At dawn the next day Leighton took his Bible and a hymn book and wandered down the driveway at Blue Water to a clump of bullrushes along the river. That morning his personal devotional life was begun. The fourteen-year-old boy saw prayer in a new and vital way. There in those Canadian woods, reading the Bible, he sensed God's voice speaking to his heart. Leighton was warmed by the assurance that his Lord was listening to his prayers. The overflow of that experience was a desire to share Christ with others. Leighton read that morning from the book of Psalms and seldom again met a new day without attuning his heart with the Infinite through the Scriptures.

Friends at school noticed a change in Leighton following his Blue Water renewal. He joined the Inter-School Christian Fellowship at Chatham Collegiate Institute and told his Christian brothers and sisters he was going to enter a public speaking contest and preach the gospel. That was a bombshell in those days when Christians were so "separated" that their presence on campus was hardly visible.

"You didn't just walk up to someone in the corridor and invite him to the youth meeting," Leighton recalled.

"We were almost a secret organization. If you wanted to invite someone you picked an individual who looked particularly vulnerable and you might invite him to a rally. You were proud to be a Christian, but you wouldn't walk down the hall and say, 'Hey, come to our youth rally this Thursday night!' "

The public speaking contest was announced and Leighton prepared feverishly. Finally his turn came and he approached the lectern of the Institute's assembly hall. Once behind the podium he threw himself into his presentation. He was a reporter at large, roaming the world, moving down the corridors of time in search of "the greatest person who ever lived." He asked historic notables of bygone eras who they thought was the greatest.

" 'Oliver Cromwell was the greatest in my day,' " he quoted someone as saying. Then Leighton would lower his voice and whisper to the audience, "But there was one who was greater."

Thus he spanned the centuries. Danny and some of the other secret Christians knew what Leighton was leading up to, but the judges had no clue. They were caught by surprise when Leighton closed his speech with: "Jesus Christ is the greatest person who ever lived." They gave him the top award. He went on to compete with Kent County high schools, giving his Christian witness in each contest.

One day as Leighton and Danny, both fifteen, were drifting homeward from school along Stanley Avenue, Leighton confided, "I've been invited to speak at the youth meeting at the First Baptist Church in Pontiac. Do you think I should?"

"Yeah, sure," Danny urged. "Take it. You'll do OK."

Several days later Leighton had his sermon ready. He preached it to Danny as they walked home from school. The theme was based on the fourth chapter of the Epistle of Paul to the Ephesians where he urged the Christians to "walk worthy" of their calling.

That first sermon was a big step. Leighton memorized his proof texts and polished every point, every gesture. When he had finished addressing the youth service in the Michigan church a freckled girl approached Leighton and said, "You sound just like Billy Graham."

"Who," Leighton had to ask, "is Billy Graham?"

Back home the milestone of his first sermon passed virtually unnoticed. Leighton's family did not have many close friends or relatives. Both parents worked in the jewelry store and he would be left alone for long stretches. When he was much younger, he awoke one night at eleven o'clock and, finding no one home, called a taxi and had the driver take him to the store in his pajamas and robe to find some companionship.

Charles and Olive Ford grew farther and farther apart, but Leighton now had the affirmation of his evangelistic calling. His mother abruptly left Chatham for six months during his fourteenth year and lived in western Canada under an assumed name. The separation healed nothing. The union that God had joined would soon be put asunder by the stubborn wills of two lonely people.

FIGHTING LONELINESS AND WINNING

Loneliness is one of the afflictions of our mobile, technological society in which relationships count for little and people are more means than ends.

Teenagers are especially lonely. They wonder if anybody understands their search for identity. University campuses can be some of the loneliest places in the world. I saw a picture of a coed in a Georgia university holding the police off with a gun and saying, "I just want someone to hug me."

Middle-aged people too can be very lonely. They face tremendous stresses of career and family. I think loneliness is what drives many housewives to alcoholism. Another pathetic sight is an older person whose children have moved away, whose friends have died, and who has no one to touch or talk to.

Loneliness for me is a kind of paradoxical experience. I have been all alone on a mountaintop and felt at peace. I have been in the midst of a busy crowd and felt terribly lonely. At times I feel a great longing for solitude. Other times I feel almost desperate for intimacy, communion, understanding.

God never intended man to be lonely. In that beautiful picture of beginnings in the Book of Genesis we see God in the evening walking with man in the cool of the Garden. What a beautiful picture of intimacy! And even with that vertical relationship with God, man was hungry for a horizontal relationship with a companion. So God said, "It is not good for man to be alone," and he created woman to stand with him heart to heart.

Sin-bred, existential loneliness—that disordered both the vertical and horizontal relationship. Man was expelled from the Garden and kept out by the angel with a great flaming sword at the entrance and man became estranged from his human companions. It wasn't long until Cain killed Abel. Sin turned man in and upon himself like an ingrown toenail. The roots of loneliness were planted in the human soul and are inherited by every person who has lived.

One of the most wonderful facets of the gospel is God's solution for loneliness. I am struck by the fact that God himself became the loneliest person in the world in order to deal with the problem. I have often thought about that awful moment when Jesus on the cross cried out, "My God, my God, why have you forsaken me?" I believe that he experienced the ultimate loneliness and then died for us so he could bring us back to God.

Christian faith is unique in the way it combines a personal and a social relationship. I have often quoted Jesus' invitation as recorded in chapter three, verse twenty of the Revelation, "Look! I have been standing at the door and I am constantly knocking. If anyone hears me calling him and opens the door, I will come in and fellowship with him and he with me."

All over the world I have seen people eating alone. It is a picture of loneliness that is stamped upon my mind. How tremendous it is to know that when we seek God's forgiveness and ask Christ to be the Lord of our lives he actually takes up residence within. He enters into a covenant to be our constant companion. And then along with that he makes us a part of God's family. When we receive Christ we also receive a lot of brothers and sisters who are committed to sharing their lives. That is one thing the church is supposed to be all about.

I don't mean that being a Christian is a magic wand that we can wave that will make loneliness vanish. The experiences of my childhood have left rough edges on my life. Even up to this time I still go through some nights of anguish when loneliness crashes like a dark wave over my soul. But I have learned that if I endure by faith, Christ will go through it with me and in the morning he will be there. Loneliness is often God's way of letting me know that it is time to reach out, to seek God's presence, and to help somebody else. Faith, hope, and love are the center of the solution. I need to believe that God is there with me, to hope that he will bring me through, and to let love impel me to think of others.

When loneliness is shared in this way it usually disappears.

5

"MR. PRESIDENT" AT FOURTEEN

In September 1945, Evon Hedley announced in Brantford that the Canadian Youth Fellowship was planning an organizational meeting to establish a rally in Chatham. Leighton seized the opportunity to host the gathering. He reserved a second-floor room in a building opposite Ford's Jewellers. At the appointed hour, he and Danny were there to welcome Hedley and a contingent of local ministers, Sunday school teachers, and youth leaders representing Fellowship Baptists, Regular Baptists, Presbyterians, The Christian and Missionary Alliance, the Pentecostal Assembly, and a collection of other groups.

After explaining what was involved, Hedley invited nominations from the floor for officers to direct the new organization. Danny, ignorant of parliamentary procedure, got to his feet. "I would like to nominate Leighton Ford for vice president."

"Danny," Evon advised, "we can't elect a *vice* president before we have a nomination for *president*."

So Danny got up again and amended his nomination: "Then I nominate Leighton for president . . . if you think he's old enough." The nomination was supported. Not until Evon returned to Brantford did he learn that the "man" who had been appointed to direct the Chatham rally was only fourteen years old. He nearly dropped over as he exclaimed to his wife, "What have I done?"

The boy director began booking Youth For Christ's top evangelists. His usherettes dressed in perky uniforms and his "Pee Wee Four Quartet" (Henry, John, and Raymond Vellinga with Jerry Russell, accompanied by Jean Cornelius) was a drawing feature. He once counted the notes in "The Flight of the Bumble Bee" which Jack Van Impe was to play on his accordion and then advertised him as "the man who can play ——— notes a second" on the accordion.

Leighton also organized rallies in surrounding towns "to awaken spiritually dead communities with the light of life." His mother bankrolled his promotional efforts. Wasn't this what she had trained him for? Youth rallies were quickly scheduled in Dresden, Wallaceburg, and Blenheim. His method was first to find pastors and lay Christians interested in supporting a rally and then to urge them to direct their own meetings, to invite speakers and to raise money for publicity and honoraria.

Hugh Deighton, a dairy and cattle farmer near Dresden, remembers his first encounter with the young evangelist who became his high school buddy: "This shiny new car pulled into our driveway during the spring thaw, and out stepped the tallest kid I ever saw. I had been hauling manure in muddy fields and was in no condition to meet city folks. But Leighton came striding over the mud with those size thirteen shoes, followed by his prim little mother who was outfitted in an expensive tailored suit. They wanted to interest me in a rally at Dresden and they wanted names of others who might also be interested in supporting a Saturday night youth rally at our church."

Hugh had been raised to be "a good boy," but he knew nothing about spiritual rebirth. He and his sister Donna shyly attended a prayer meeting which Leighton arranged. Two weeks later Hugh found himself sitting in a business meeting of Youth For Christ rally directors.

"As we talked and shared our thoughts about the purpose of the Dresden rally I was born again right there in the circle," Hugh says. "Through Leighton's prodding I went to work—singing in the glee club, leading in prayer, and finally taking over our local rally as director for five years."

Youth For Christ Magazine was *the* periodical to be read. In it Leighton learned about the big Winona Lake, Indiana, YFC conference and in July he was there with Bible, note pads, and movie camera. At fifteen, Leighton stood six feet four inches tall, wore size thirteen shoes, and weighed 135 pounds.

Winona was a heady experience. There he met Torrey Johnson, cofounder of Youth For Christ; Bob Pierce, YFC's "laughing boy" until he went to Asia and returned with a broken heart for wasted humanity; Bob Cook, Chuck Templeton, Peter Deyneka, Armin Gesswein, and others. At a meeting of YFC directors in which Leighton was asked to take the minutes, he first shook hands with the man he was said to resemble in his preaching style. Billy Graham did most of the talking at the meeting. He joked about being arrested in Canada. A storm-tossed plane in which he was riding across British Columbia had been forced down in a field and passengers were booked into a local hotel. That night, police raided Billy's room and placed him under arrest until it could be established that the evangelist had no connection with the suspected bank robber with whom he had shared a room.

Leighton attended every prayer meeting in the Rainbow Room of the Westminster Hotel where long nights of prayer frequently heard the yearning supplications of these men who thirsted after spiritual power. Their goals for world evangelization later surfaced in the global impact of both the Berlin World Congress on Evangelism and the International Congress on World Evangelization in Lausanne, Switzerland. Leighton listened raptly to Harold John Ockenga in the Billy Sunday Tabernacle and was curious about how he gave an invitation—something the Canadian Bible conference preachers seldom did. He walked to the front of that auditorium and prayed aloud with the gathered crowd: "Lord, send me." In his diary Leighton wrote: "God broke me. . . . I have discovered slightly how proud I am. I love to stand before men. My own ambition for a big place is spoiling me for God. I trust His Spirit shall truly put me in my place. . . ."

Leighton learned at the 1948 Winona Lake conference that Billy Graham was planning to itinerate throughout Ontario, so he booked him for a January 1949 rally in Chatham. Billy was known for his skill in giving an invitation. Having Graham in Chatham would be a smashing event even then—nine months before the world heard of "Gabriel in Gabardine," a phrase coined by the press when Billy rocketed to fame during his September 1949 Los Angeles crusade.

In those early days Billy didn't ease into his sermons with introductory niceties. Instead he leaped to the podium with his tongue already engaged:

"Philosophy says *think* again; education says *teach* again; psychology says *try* again, but the Bible says be *born* again!"

Billy bounded off the plane at Windsor to greet Leighton and a small band of Canadians who had braved snow and ice to meet him that frigid January afternoon.

"Everything is ready but the weather," Leighton reported en route through the storm to his home where Billy was made comfortable. "But we expect this to be our biggest rally."

The program participants were almost as numerous as the audience that night. Ed Darling, director of Detroit's "Voice of Christian Youth," brought a contingent. The Ohman Brothers' Trumpet Trio from Cleveland, Ohio, joined local talent which Leighton had worked into the program. As the hour grew later it was apparent that the spectacular offered too much music for Chatham's big night.

Billy preached on the subject, "Prepare, O Israel, to meet thy God." He pointed out two choices—either meet the Lord in life as Savior or meet him in death as judge. Leighton watched the audience hopefully. The invitation . . . every head bowed . . . one person walked to the platform. Probably only believers had braved the storm. Billy prayed. The exits of the auditorium were opened. The evangelistic extravaganza had ended disappointingly.

Leighton slipped over to a wing of the stage and cried. Billy followed and put his arm around him. "Leighton, God has given you a burden and he always blesses a man with a burden."

Leighton squared his shoulders and looked at Billy. "Maybe the harvest will come later," he said to the man he most admired.

Outside, the forces of winter raged, icing the naked trees and filling up roadways with snow. Leighton's mother served hot soup and a snack to their distinguished company.

"What are your plans for college?" Billy asked in the ornate dining room of the Ford's large house on Tecumseh Park.

"I am enrolled in the University of Toronto and afterward I guess I'll get some theological training at Knox College."

Billy ate quietly, deep in thought. "Have you thought about Wheaton College?"

Leighton had read J. Wesley Ingles' novel *The Silver Trumpet* and knew of the school in suburban Chicago from which Billy had graduated six years earlier.

"Would the registrar send me a brochure this late?"

Billy lent his endorsement and that fall Leighton entered the alma mater of his admired friend, one week before Billy Graham was catapulted to international fame during his tent meeting at Washington and Hill Streets in Los Angeles in September 1949.

Canadian snow kept falling that night and all departing planes were grounded. After finishing the snack Billy was driven to the Chatham train station. Instead of flying to Ottawa on the wings of a plane, Billy had to sit up on a train, whistle-stopping through the night all the way to Ontario's capital city.

Before leaving Chatham for college Leighton asked his pastor, Scott Fulton, if he might join the First Presbyterian Church. McKenzie Ross, clerk of the session that year, called together eight elders to hear the seventeen-year-old's confession of faith. Chairman Ross remembers that Leighton stood before them in a snappy jacket, sporty pants, and white shoes. The elders were satisfied with what they called his "clear, sharp answers" to all questions and they admitted Leighton into the membership of the church.

The gray Olds was loaded for the trip that would take Leighton to Illinois, farther from home than he had ever traveled. Mrs. Ford insisted on going along and further embarrassed her son by renting an apartment near the campus to keep an eye on him.

PREPARATION

"Be sure to use the abilities God has given you through his prophets when the elders of the church laid their hands upon your head" (1 Tim. 4:14).

Following campus tradition, Leighton and Jean (right) rang the Wheaton College tower bell to announce their engagement. The author, Norman Rohrer, is at the bottom center of the picture. Behind Jean is Clayton Bell, brother of Mrs. Billy Graham, and his fiancée, Peggy.

6

WHEATON

All achievers have had their mentors by whom they have honed their faculties to embrace truths great and small. Leighton Ford had Wheaton College, where he joined a student body of 1,500 dedicated to the pursuit of knowledge "for Christ and His Kingdom."

Wheaton has been described as the evangelicals' Harvard. Founded in 1860 as The Illinois Institute, the school stands today among liberal arts schools of the highest accreditation. All who entered with Leighton in 1949 signed a pledge of total abstinence from tobacco, liquor, and movie-going. Mrs. Ford, watching from her post off-campus, found the movie ban curious. Her austere conservatism could match anybody's, but she had not struck movies off her list of permissibles. She tugged occasionally on the apron strings from her watchtower while Leighton tried to keep her clinging presence a secret. Finally he was able to assure Olive that academia only strengthened his resolve to preach and she returned to Chatham.

Wheaton was a daily serendipity for the young preacher. His room was only a few blocks from the international headquarters of Youth For Christ where his heroes came and went. Gil Dodds, world champion indoor miler, was Wheaton's track coach; a school friend named Bill Davies was the brother of nationally famous basketball star Bob Davies, who had embraced the Christian faith. How different was all this from the secretive Christian front in Chatham schools!

His Canadian high school had given Leighton the equivalent of his first year of college so he entered

Wheaton as a sophomore at seventeen. He felt socially awkward and shy, but almost from the first day on campus he had a steady girl in red-haired Elaine Severin from Grosse Pointe, Michigan. He had met the clarinet player when she visited Chatham that spring with the Wheaton College band.

The second semester was opened on February 5, 1950, with "spiritual emphasis week" led by the Rev. Edwin Johnson of Seattle. Examinations had dampened campus spirit and even though President V. Raymond Edman signed all communiques "Cheerily," the gray winter days tended to make the students anything but. Few expected more than routine chapel services during "spiritual emphasis week."

In that first meeting Pastor Ed took as his text: 2 Chronicles 7:14. The following night one after another student rose to share some personal victory or to confess sin. Finally there were so many students standing that Prexy invited them to the choir loft in Pierce Chapel to take their turn at the microphone. They confessed pride, bad attitudes, a variety of carnal sins, and occasionally theft.

On Tuesday, February 7, Leighton wrote an open letter to friends of Youth For Christ in Chatham: "I personally did not expect anything wonderful to happen but somehow on that first night the feeling came to me that this was it." •

On Wednesday, February 8, "it" took the school by surprise. Spiritual revival electrified the campus and touched the hearts of most students. There was singing in the chow lines. Students asked forgiveness of those they had wronged; grudges were settled; items missing from gym lockers were returned; open confessions indicated that the sin of pride transcended all other transgressions. Chicago newspapers headlined the thirty-eight-hour revival; *Life* magazine's February 20, 1950, edition carried a double spread; students began traveling to churches in northern Illinois to share what had happened.

In a six-page letter home Leighton confessed: "Many times back in Chatham I unkindly spoke about many Christians and groups in the city; I need forgiveness for that. . . . I saw myself as God must see me. For the first time in my life God really stripped me of my sham and let me see the blackness in the recesses of my heart. . . ."

After the Wheaton College revival Leighton was drawn into a circle of the committed known informally as the campus preacher boys. I was among them. In late afternoons we gathered in an upper room prayer meeting above the odor of sweating bodies and steaming showers in Alumni Gym. There John Wesley White, Tedd Seelye, Pete Deyneka Jr., Dick Shrout, Frank Nelsen, Murray Marshall, Leighton Ford, and I poured out our supplications.

In a moment of commitment following one of those impassioned sessions, Shrout stood up and declared: "I would give up anything for God. In fact, I wish I had a girl friend just so I could give her up for God!" Having none, he then proposed that he quit school and get on with the work of evangelization. We persuaded him to stay in school and graduate with his class.

Leighton was, to my mind, the leader of that devoted band. Our hearts beat to serve God. In our zeal we became campus ascetics, I'm afraid. We spurned girls and imagined ourselves to be storm troopers in the vanguard of the King's army.

Many thought that Leighton had copied Billy Graham's style of preaching. The similarities were explainable: both were tall (Leighton is nearly an inch taller than Billy) and thin (Leighton runs ten pounds lighter than his brother-in-law but is an inch broader in the shoulders). Both have the same voice characteristics. Both have expansive gesticulation, a commanding voice, an urgency of theme. And both were caught up in the fervor of the new Youth For Christ movement that demanded such a flamboyant style.

Our zeal embraced the world. Before school ended in 1950 we commissioned John Wesley White to "win the European continent for Christ." I think he was joining a YFC-sponsored preaching tour of some sort. On his departing day John met the commuter train wearing bright green pants, a cream sport jacket and an outlandish straw hat. He was ready! We encircled him and prayed that God would use our brother "as a firebrand for proclaiming the good news in all of Europe." Tedd Seelye remembers that Leighton stepped back, took another look at John, and probably tried to picture him getting off the plane in London wearing that headgear. Suddenly he wrestled it away from John and stashed it into a trash can. John let it go, but I'm sure it pained him to see his dapper chapeau lying crumpled on a train platform.

While John White was in Europe that summer of 1950, Leighton headed east with a team of his own including piano player Wendell Babcock and trombonist Bill Elliot Jr. Leighton preached his four polished sermons all across Ohio, Pennsylvania, and the Canadian Maritime Provinces, where they traveled in a new Buick sedan his parents had given him. The sameness of those sermons grew tedious with each dramatic retelling. Tensions built. Wendell felt that Leighton didn't prepare properly for each new meeting. Bill accused Leighton of not taking proper care of the automobile his parents had bought him.

Bill could point to the night when they left a small country church in New Brunswick during a rainstorm to get a head start on the next day's journey. The car was new and Leighton sliced through the water at a good clip. Suddenly the road divided. Was it because he is left-handed that Leighton veered to the left onto a muddy, rain-soaked unpaved road, splashing water and mud like a

cavorting rhinoceros? Instead of slowing down and stop-
ping, he accelerated, as if to fly somehow above the
muddy prison of those ruts. No amount of pushing could
dislodge the car. They had gone as far as they could go
that night. When the sun rose the trio unwound themselves from sleep and brushed off muddy shoes. Someone
wandered off and located a farmer who pulled them out
with a tractor.

By the time the trio ended the tour they were all
peeved. Small personal rivalries had arisen. Leighton admitted he had been "inconsiderate, demanding, stand-
offish with a lot to learn."

That fall he tried again. His second team included
Peter Deyneka Jr. and myself with our trombones. It
seemed as though in the two years that followed we sang
"Let's Be True to Jesus" a thousand times. Later bass
soloist Bob Schindler was added "to give the team some
class."

We criss-crossed the Midwest and penetrated such
states as the Carolinas, Georgia, Florida, and Tennessee.
And of course we visited Billy and Ruth Graham in Montreat, North Carolina.

On November 5, 1950, somewhere along Route 30 in
Illinois we pulled to the side and listened raptly to the
first "Hour of Decision" broadcast by Billy. Leighton
could not have known then that his own voice would one
day be regularly heard on that program, alternating every
other week with Billy's.

By 1952 Mrs. Ford had moved to Toronto, leaving in
Chatham a bitter and lonely husband. Mr. Ford often
took a train or a plane to our meetings. He seemed eager
to hear his son preach. At the close of Leighton's sermon
in a Miami Beach Presbyterian Church, Charles Ford
raised his hand in response to the invitation to receive
Christ. Afterward we left father and son alone so they
could enjoy the sacred moment together. Memories of
their divided home must have pained them. Their re-

union in Christ that night was in reality a kind of reunion with their confused and troubled wife and mother living far to the north in a pinched and fearful existence.

God reminded us occasionally on those trips that the breath of life we all enjoyed was held by a delicate thread. One moonless, winter night we were returning to campus from an assignment in Wisconsin. I was at the wheel of Leighton's car, westbound on Highway 64 only a few miles north of Wheaton. Suddenly an island of ice appeared on the crest of the road. I took my foot off the accelerator and eased to the right, not braking for fear of a skid. The car veered back to the left and I corrected . . . then right and I corrected again. Farther left . . . farther right, twisting crazily until we had spun completely around. Then . . . Wham! The back wheels climbed an embankment on the right side.

In the sudden quiet Leighton led us in a prayer of thanksgiving for the blessing of survival. When our eyes grew accustomed to the darkness we saw that hardly thirty feet ahead stood an ugly cement bulkhead for a drainage canal. I started the engine, the fellows pushed, and the car leaped right out again onto the road. The only casualty was a left rear wheel that had been slightly bent. Leighton didn't get it fixed, and so we wobbled all the way to Florida and back that Easter. Like Jacob's dislocated hip joint, the wheel reminded us of God's intervention on a dark night in a snowy ditch.

In 1951 Leighton became a candidate for student body president during his senior year. He persuaded a reluctant Sam Befus to manage his campaign and the stage was set. Ford buttons blossomed. His campaign slogan was: "There's a Ford in your future." Posters showed a boy and a girl—the girl poised for a kiss, the boy admiring instead a passing Ford car. It was the wrong poster for conservative Wheatonites in the early fifties.

In his campaign speech at chapel he was advised to be cool, to play down his preacher status, to appeal for votes in a reasoned, logical manner. His opponent, Elmer Wolfenden, roared to the podium flashing a broad smile. A banner screaming "Wolfenden for President" was unfurled. Applause greeted his opening line. Wolfenden was launched.

Leighton and Sam erected a sign outside a concert hall on which gasoline-soaked rags spelled "Ford." Just as Wheatonites flocked out of the building the "bomb" was lit. The smoking inferno put Leighton's campaign further behind. Next step: an endorsement from an off-campus figure that wrinkled noses and sent more voters into Wolfenden's lair. The Ford campaign grew steadily worse. Every trick backfired. In the runoff Leighton got one more vote than in the primary and Elmer took the election. Leighton tried to be brave but the stinging defeat hurt. He was accustomed to winning, not losing. But he would run again for office in seminary and things would go better without the "wolf" on his trail.

Leighton Ford arrested on the campus of Wheaton College?

Roy Aldrich, who lived on the same floor with him in the Howard Fisher residence on Michigan Avenue, had accumulated a large assortment of trash which Leighton helped load into the Buick for a trip to the dump. They cruised around on a back road near Herrick's Lake looking without success for a remote trash heap.

"Why not into the lake?" Roy suggested.

Leighton backed up and popped open the trunk lid. Just as they had finished polluting the muddy lake a deputy sheriff approached. He looked at the light bulbs, the soggy notebooks, and the test papers floating on the water and commanded, "You have this stuff out of here by tomorrow or else."

Back on campus the lake was forgotten. The boys thought the stuff would sink quickly to the bottom and disappear. The word "ecology" was unknown then. They were in the gym when a phone call from Dean Brooks asked Leighton Ford and Roy Aldrich to appear in his office immediately and explain a warrant for their arrest. The dean persuaded the officer to let him handle it and the case of the polluted lake was resolved through a lawyer who arranged for a littering fine.

So easily done! So painlessly. Leighton had been well looked after at home; he was being well looked after at school; later he would be well looked after in his work. Persons in positions of leadership become accustomed to a world that revolves around them and their plans.

Other practical matters were to be learned in the halls of alma mater. Leighton prayed—sometimes desperately—that he might be "approved of God, meet for the Master's use, prepared unto every good work."

Leighton's nimble mind was a seed bed for the postulations of such professors as Merrill Tenney, Arthur Holmes, Kenneth Kantzer and Clarence Hale. Classmate John Wesley White, in his best preacher parlance, describes Leighton's "joint capacities both for immense comprehension and for the ability to articulate his convictions with precise accuracy and compelling forcefulness." He found in Leighton "a felicitous combination of those evasive personality chemistries of humanity, humility, and humor. He knows the right mixtures of wit, simplicity, and pathos to deal with nearly any variety of situation. . . ."

Translated, this means (I think) that Leighton was qualified to enter upon his college major in philosophy. He proved it by graduating with the highest score on his comprehensive examinations of all other students in Wheaton's ninety-two-year history.

DEALING WITH DOUBT

A *magazine article entitled, "The Doubting American—a Growing Breed," noted that pessimism, distrust of leaders, and laxity in moral standards all raised a basic question: Whatever happened to belief? Yet along with the loss of faith, says the article, there is evidence of "a stubborn yearning for basic faith."*

A great British preacher was asked what changes he noticed in people over his lifetime. He answered that a half century ago in any congregation the preacher could count on a general sense of guilt, but now the only thing he can count on is a general sense of doubt!

Some happy souls seem to live in a kind of perpetual spiritual sunshine, with a simple faith, and never a doubt. I envy them! There are others for whom doubt is a chronic affliction, who are constantly buffeted with questions that seem to have no answer. I have compassion for them. And then there are those who are in between—who generally have buoyant times of faith and sunshine, but are sometimes afflicted by spiritual clouds and rain. I identify with them!

Based on my own experience there are several things that I would like to say to a person who has a problem with doubt, whether it is occasional or chronic. First, you are not alone! Doubt is not uncommon. John Bunyan, who wrote Pilgrim's Progress, *was afflicted all his life with the fear that he had committed the unpardonable sin. The outstanding Latin American missionary statesman, Kenneth Strachan, was tormented by crippling doubts toward the end of his life. I believe there are many people who never really have a doubt . . . but I would say to them, "Remember there are some of us—and I am one—for whom doubt is sometimes a problem!"*

Then I would like to say: Your doubt is not sin. Doubt is a particular kind of intellectual temptation. The sin is not in being tempted but in yielding to it. There is a basic difference between doubt and unbelief. Doubt has a problem with believing. Doubt says, "I can't believe but I want to," or, "I would like to believe but I have problems." Unbelief on the other hand, is willful refusal to believe—even to face the evidence. Doubt says, "I can't." Unbelief says, "I won't," or "I don't want to." Doubt is typified by the man who said to Jesus, "Lord, I believe, help my unbelief." Willful unbelief is described by Paul in Romans 1, where he tells us the wrath of God is revealed from heaven against the wickedness of men "who push away the truth from them" (Rom. 1:18). Paul points out that there is plenty of evidence that this class of unbeliever does not want to believe—he doesn't want it to interfere with his ego-centered life style.

The third piece of advice: Your doubt can be of value. Doubt can be a trial that makes your faith stronger. A faith that has never been tested or assaulted by doubt is a faith that can be very vulnerable and fragile. But if you have thought, prayed, battled your way through doubt you can end up with a stronger faith. You may doubt that an airplane can carry you safely—and your doubts will linger unless you actually face them and get on the aircraft and find out what it can do. Students who enter college never having faced problems and difficulties with their faith may be much more susceptible to hostile attacks on their Christianity from unbelieving friends and professors than those who have had to face the problems earlier.

Peter's words about sufferings and trials can be applied to doubt. "These trials are only to test your faith, to see whether or not it is strong and pure" (1 Pet. 1:7). So, if you are passing through a period of doubt don't reject it, be thankful for it even if it is uncomfortable.

Finally, realize that your doubt can be dealt with. I am impressed when I see how Jesus dealt with doubters. When John the Baptist, who had announced Jesus' coming, was thrown into prison he was filled with doubt. He sent some of his followers to Jesus to ask, "Are you really the one we are waiting for, or shall we keep on looking?" His circumstances cast him into doubt.

How could Jesus really be the Messiah when John was in prison? Jesus dealt with John in compassion, honesty, and challenge. He did not rebuke or condemn him for having questions. He pointed to the evidence—"the blind people I've healed, and the lame people now walking without help, . . . and the deaf who hear . . . and my preaching the Good News to the poor." And then he gave John a challenge, "Blessed are those who don't doubt me" (Matt. 11:3-6).

Similarly, the well known disciple "doubting Thomas" was not convinced that Jesus had actually been raised from the dead. He had not been there when Jesus appeared to the other disciples and told them, "I won't believe it unless I see the nail wounds in his hands—and put my finger into them—and place my hand in his side" (John 20:25). Shortly afterward, Jesus appeared again to the disciples and Thomas was with them. Once again he didn't condemn Thomas for his doubt. He pointed to the evidence, and gave the challenge, "Put your finger into my hands," he said. "Put your hand into my side. Don't be faithless any longer. Believe!" Thomas said to him, "My Lord and my God."

When Jesus dealt with doubters he avoided the extreme attitude of condemnation on the one hand or sentimentality on the other. He faced their doubts honestly. He told them to look at the evidence. He challenged them to an attitude of faith.

So my suggestions as to handling doubt are these:

Be honest about your doubt. Don't hide it from yourself and most of all from God. After all, if God is really there, he already knows about your doubt. Have you ever thought of coming to God and saying honestly, "God, I really want to believe but I have these doubts and I want you to help me to deal with them"? If we just try to suppress our doubts, it drains a tremendous amount of spiritual energy and is even more corrosive of our faith.

Then try to analyze your doubt. Where does it come from? What is it rooted in? Some doubt grows out of genuine intellectual questionings of Christianity. We may have questions about the deity of Christ, or the possibility of miracles, or the accu-

racy of the Scripture, because of challenges that have been thrown at us.

Some doubt is rooted in disobedience. When we are stubbornly pursuing our way in known sin or rebellion we are likely to find that our minds project doubt. We don't want to believe because if we really believed we would have to change our behavior.

Some doubt comes from our "moods." Often we are perplexed that after a great spiritual "high" a period of doubt sets in. This may be due simply to emotional, physical, or spiritual exhaustion. Elijah, the prophet in the Old Testament, confronted the false prophets of Baal and had a showdown on Mount Carmel in which he and they prayed for the true God to reveal himself by fire. The true and living Lord God whom Elijah served revealed himself by sending a great stroke of fire from heaven which consumed the sacrifice on the altar and all the people fell down and said, "The Lord is God." It was a tremendous display of God's power. But immediately after, Elijah went into a period of gloom and despair and asked God to take his life because he felt he was the only one who was really dedicated. Elijah had been so involved and caught up in what was happening that the pendulum had to swing and a reaction set in.

So periods of doubt can arise out of our emotional mood-swings. At other times doubt can be a pervasive, existential feeling of numbness and unreality . . . for which there seems to be no particular cause, but which overwhelms us like a great flood.

In order to sort out and get rid of our doubt, it often helps to share it with someone else, to talk it out both with God in prayer—and with a trusted friend or Christian counselor. When we bury the sense of doubt within ourselves it can grow so great that we lose our perspective. A good friend or counselor can help us to get outside ourselves and to look at doubt more realistically.

Look for answers and ways of dealing with doubt. If you have a particular problem intellectually don't ignore it; look for the answers. When I was in college I wondered whether the Scrip-

tures were trustworthy. But I found that there were many books which gave solid answers to these questions. I also found that my belief was strengthened when I learned, for example, that archaeological discoveries have again and again confirmed the historical accuracy of the Scriptures.

I had problems about the claims of Jesus Christ. Was he really the Son of God or was this simply a teaching that had been foisted on me by my parents and Sunday school teachers? As I read and examined the claims of Jesus himself and faced the evidence, I realized that his claims were beyond those of a mere man. I had to decide—was he a liar who claimed to be the Son of God when he wasn't? Was he a lunatic who was self-deluded? Or was he really the Lord? I came to the conclusion that he was the Christ, the Son of the Living God. To work through my doubt I had to face the questions. I discovered that there were solid answers.

When doubt is caused by disobedience then the only thing we can do is to face honestly that rebellious area of our lives and be willing to change by God's power. When doubt is caused by an emotional mood swing, perhaps what we need most of all is not to study but to change our pace. God took Elijah when the prophet was discouraged and put him to sleep, gave him cool water from a brook, fed him by food brought by ravens. . . . Only after his servant was completely rested did God give him a new revelation of himself.

It is more difficult when it seems that God withdraws himself and a great mood of doubt overshadows our whole spiritual landscape. The only answer I know of at that time is to be patient with God, with ourselves, and with our doubt and to believe that God will bring us through.

Dr. Edman, who was president of Wheaton College when I was there as a student, used to say, "When you are on a train and you come into a dark tunnel, even though you can't see anything you don't jump off the train! You hold onto your ticket and you trust the engineer."

The writer of Hebrews told some Christians who were going through real suffering and were tempted to doubt, "Do not let this happy trust in the Lord die away, no matter what happens. Remember your reward! You need to keep on patiently doing God's will if you want him to do for you all that he has promised. His coming will not be delayed much longer. And those whose faith has made them good in God's sight must live by faith, trusting him in everything. Otherwise, if they shrink back, God will have no pleasure in them. But we have never turned our backs on God and sealed our fate. No, our faith in him assures our souls' salvation" (Heb. 10:35-39).

Several times in my life I have gone through periods of deep doubt. One of these occurred in the late sixties when we were preparing for an evangelistic campaign in Seattle, Washington. Preparations were difficult and discouraging. I remember flying home from Seattle and at some point on that flight it seemed as if God just disappeared. I felt that he just wasn't even there anymore. It became so bad that I decided I would have to leave the ministry if it continued. How could I continue to preach honestly if I didn't believe that God was there? I went so far as to begin wondering what my associates and colleagues would do if our Team had to break up. I cried out desperately for God to help but in the "dark night of the soul" there seemed to be no reply.

The answer came in two ways. I remember sitting up almost all of one night with my wife, Jeanie. She listened as I poured out my woe and sense of desolation. We talked for hours. She listened sympathetically as I shared the problem I was facing, but she was wise enough not to let me drown in self-pity. Just to pour all of this out and to have her understanding and love and strength was of tremendous help.

The other thing that helped me was to look outside myself and to realize that my faith was based not just on my own internal feeling but on external evidence. How did anything get here in the first place? I wondered. It made more sense to accept by faith that the universe was formed by the word and will of God than that the whole thing was a meaningless chaos. Again and again I came back to the bedrock of Christianity: the resurrection of Jesus Christ from the dead. If Christ's tomb was empty, and the stone was rolled away, and if his disciples were transformed by seeing him (as was Thomas), regardless of what my emotions were at that time, there was solid ground on which I would be able to walk again.

Slowly I learned to doubt my doubts and believe my beliefs. The deep, dark clouds that had wrapped around my soul were blown away by the fresh winds of God's spirit and I learned to walk in his light again. I believe the result was faith that was stronger, and more effective, and more understanding of others because of the trial of doubt that God had brought me through.

1953: Rehearsal for the wedding of Leighton Ford and Jean Graham. From left to right: Grady Wilson, George Beverly Shea, Leighton Ford, Cliff Barrows, Billy Graham.

7

COLUMBIA

The Wheaton College Crusaders had the basketball and were lurching down the court toward the net. The crowd erupted as the ball zipped through the orange-and-blue strings, detonating the roar of victory.

"There he is!" a classmate whispered, punching Jean Graham in the ribs. *"Down there selling popcorn."*

"Who you talkin' about?"

"You know, Leighton Ford—the guy who sounds like your brother when he preaches."

Jean Coffey Graham, a petite blonde sophomore from Charlotte, North Carolina, saw that night the man who would become her husband. She was not impressed, but she soon had a chance to see him up close. John White took Jean to see the Blackhawks play hockey in Chicago and invited Leighton and another girl as a double date. John and Leighton had plotted the whole thing so Leighton could get a look at Billy Graham's sister.

"I was flattered by Leighton's attention that night," Jean said, "not realizing the date was a setup."

She was less impressed when Leighton came thirty minutes late for their first campus date. Jean had decided he'd forgotten both her and the concert and was heading for the library when Leighton bounded into the lobby of North Hall Dorm. "Sorry I'm late," he apologized. "Could you . . ."

"Be back in a minute."

They were too late to find seats together at the concert. Afterward he took her home thirty minutes after curfew and the dorm mother issued a grounding for one week.

"What do you *think* of him?" her roommates chorused when Jean stepped into the second-floor hallway.

"Well," Jean mused, "he wasn't so much fun but he's different from any other guy I've ever dated." She selected a hanger and stowed her coat in her closet. "And I don't expect I'll ever date him again," she added.

On their second date Leighton took her to hear Evangelist Percy Crawford at Chicago's Gospel Tabernacle. En route back to campus they stopped on North Avenue at an all-night drive-in for two large orange drinks. As Leighton brought the drinks to the little round table their eyes met in a new way. He looked at her, she looked at him and they both knew absolutely that this was it. But they didn't share this certainty for perhaps a year and a half.

After graduation Leighton spent the summer showing the film *Mr. Texas* in churches of six states, trying all the while to make up his mind about which theological seminary to enter. Knox College in Toronto? His mother wanted that. Princeton? His Presbyterian counselors wanted that. Columbia Theological Seminary in Decatur, Georgia? Jean would like that. He was in love with a Southern girl. Besides, the institution of the Presbyterian (Southern) Church was then among the more conservative of ministerial boot camps. Columbia would be the one. He was admitted in September 1952, a couple of weeks before classes began, settling into the room once occupied by the celebrated chaplain of the U.S. Senate, Peter Marshall.

At Columbia Leighton consociated with both liberals and conservatives. Nearly every campus, theological, and denominational issue was argued from the two viewpoints. One evening Leighton sat listening to a cluster of conservative students raking liberals over the coals for pushing union between the northern Presbyterian Church U.S.A. with the southern Presbyterian Church

U.S. The pro-unionist liberals were being cut down verbally and lampooned.

"It occurs to me," Leighton interrupted, "that if our theology is so much better than theirs then the fruit of our theology—love—should also be better than theirs. And I wonder how much of that we are demonstrating by our actions and by our words."

The evangelical tenets Leighton took to Columbia held firm. The dean who had curled his lip, thinking Wheaton was a second-rate Bible school, was amazed to find that his new student knew more technical philosophy than any classmate. Years later that same man flew to Charlotte to ask Leighton to direct a major evangelistic program of the Presbyterian Church U.S.

Leighton knew Greek so well that he sometimes corrected a professor's errors at the chalk board. He also wanted to master the Hebrew language, so he enrolled in the class of a professor who ought to have retired years before. The man was exceedingly weary of teaching his subject and often would stop right in the middle of class, slump over on his desk, and exclaim, "Over forty years! I'm sick of it! Sick of it!"

Others didn't mind this diversion but Leighton seemed to. He wanted to learn Hebrew, and he was annoyed by any delay in getting the complicated language into his mind. He also wanted to maintain his 4.0 grade average. The professor would often spend half an hour discussing an issue from a liberal perspective then thirty minutes apologizing for it. By then the bell would ring and the class would leave, happy that they had once again followed the line of least resistance. Not Leighton. He would be obviously miffed by the digression.

Leighton played basketball for the seminary team. He also liked to wrestle classmate Calvin Thielman, a wiry Texan who had grown up in a family of seven children on a cotton ranch.

"I can still remember his face turning red," says Calvin laughing. "It looked as though a vessel in his face would break. He put up a good scuffle, but he was just too skinny."

Calvin and Leighton were campus inseparables. Each Saturday evening when the seminary kitchen dispensed sack lunches they would drive downtown "to find something decent to eat." They would also scan the newspapers searching for good preaching in nearby Sunday pulpits. Sometimes they would drive as many as a hundred and sixty-five miles to hear someone preach or to fill a pulpit themselves.

Leighton was married halfway through his second year in seminary. The sister of Billy Graham was a curiosity to Columbians. Jeanie kept house in a first-story seminary room with bathroom facilities down the hall shared by three other couples. She worked at the Billy Graham Film Office in Atlanta and went with Leighton to intern at Westminster Presbyterian Church, Springfield, Missouri, for a summer.

Occasionally Leighton was kidded about his reserved manners and his speech distinctions. He says "kote" for "quote," and "vare" for "very." "Rather" comes out *"rah*-ther," with of course the Canadian "nigh-ther" and "eye-ther" for "neither" and "either." In addition, his "th" sound in words like "through" is not a complete stop, sounding more like "t" with a slight escape of air. "Also" is pronounced "altso."

In early winter during Leighton's final semester at Columbia in 1955, a letter arrived from Billy Graham: "We are leaving this spring for extensive meetings in the British Isles. I would like you and Jean to join us for evangelistic crusades and preaching missions in Scotland. Let me know as soon as you can."

Leighton took the letter to Seminary President J. McDowell Richards. "It does seem like an unusually good opportunity," Dr. Richards agreed, "but school doesn't end until late in May."

"If I took my exams six weeks early. . . ."

Dr. Richards smiled. "Perhaps it can be arranged."

The balance of the semester's work was outlined and Leighton studied ahead. Shortly after Easter he wrote his senior examinations then left with Jean for Europe. He scored higher than any other man in class and was graduated *magna cum laude* and *in absentia*. Leighton was twenty-three years old. A new door of evangelistic opportunity had opened. He entered it with the enthusiasm of youth.

Counseling young people is an important part of Leighton Ford's ministry.

THERE IS A GIFT FOR YOU

Jeanie and I were sitting by the pond at the Willow Valley Farms Hotel near Lancaster, Pennsylvania—Norm Rohrer's home town—where I was conducting evangelistic services. Our eyes were caught by the fascinating competition of a goose trying to keep several ducks out of the small lake. We were struck by the contrast between the style of the ducks on land and in water. When they were trying to run from the goose on land the ducks were ungainly, wobbly, awkward, and rather ridiculous. But in their natural element of water they were immediately transformed into beautifully graceful creatures.

We let our imaginations run away: why didn't someone start a school to teach ducks to run? Or rabbits to swim? Or turtles to fly? It would be such a ridiculous misunderstanding of the gifts that God had given to each of these special and unique animals.

And then we reflected how awkward and out-of-place many Christians are because they have never discovered the uniqueness of the spiritual gifts God has given to them. Many sincere Christians have a tremendous dedication and they desperately seek to arrive at some kind of spiritual fulfillment but they never quite make it in their own minds. All their lives they have felt "out-of-place." Part of the reason is that they haven't grasped the plan that God has for spiritual gifts.

Along with the free gift of salvation (Eph. 2:8, 9) God also gives to every believer in Jesus Christ a special ministering or serving gift. A "spiritual gift" is a special ability which God gives to Christians to serve God and to help build up the Church, the Body of Christ. These spiritual gifts may or may not be related to our natural talents.

In recent years a number of books have been written on the subject of spiritual gifts, by Bible teachers who estimate that there may be as many as twenty-five to thirty spiritual gifts mentioned in the New Testament. These gifts range from the speaking gifts (preaching and teaching) to the serving gifts (hospitality, liberality, administration), to the more spectacular—and controversial—"sign" gifts (healing, speaking in tongues, interpreting). Some of the New Testament passages which deal with these gifts in detail include Romans 12; Ephesians 4; 1 Corinthians 12 and 14.

To be useful, fulfilled, and happy in our Christian lives we need to know and practice the will of God. That is basic. Romans 12 is a classic passage that shows how finding and doing the will of God requires both a willingness to do God's will and an understanding of how our spiritual gifts fit into God's master plan. In this passage Paul urges his Christian brothers, in view of God's mercy, "to give your bodies to God. Let them be a living sacrifice, holy—the kind he can accept . . ." and to be "a new and different person with a fresh newness in all you do and think" (Rom. 12:1, 2). Then, he promises, "You will learn from your own experience how his ways will really satisfy you." Yet I have met many Christians who, as sincerely as they know how, have offered themselves to God in this way and have asked him to renew their minds and still feel that they haven't discovered what the will of God is.

The problem may be that they have stopped with those first two verses and haven't gone on to Paul's further teaching in the verses that follow. There Paul urges Christians not to think too highly of themselves but to think realistically of themselves and to understand the measure of faith God has given to them. He points out, "Just as there are many parts to our bodies, so it is with Christ's body. We are all parts of it, and it takes every one of us to make it complete, for we each have different work to do. So we belong to each other, and each needs all the others. God has given each of us the ability to do certain things well. So if God has given you the ability to prophesy, then prophesy whenever you can—as often as your faith is strong enough to receive a message from God. If your gift is that of serving others, serve them well. If you are a teacher, do a good job of teaching. If you are a preacher, see to it that your sermons are strong and helpful. *If God has given you money, be generous in helping others with it. If God has given you administrative ability and put you in charge of the work of others, take the responsibility seriously. Those who offer comfort to the sorrowing should do so with Christian cheer."* (Rom. 12:4-8).

My friend Peter Wagner has pointed out that to *"learn from your own experience how his ways will satisfy you"* involves both "consecration" theology, and "gift" theology. In other words, it is not enough just to offer our bodies and minds to God, to consecrate ourselves in that general way. The consecration must become specific through understanding, appropriating, and using that particular spiritual gift that God has given to each of us for the good of Christ's Body. Without an attitude of sincere consecration, spiritual gifts are hollow and meaningless. But without an understanding of our gifts, consecration is nebulous, impractical, and unfulfilling.

Perhaps we should ask the question: *"Do we see our place of service as a 'totem pole' or as a 'body'?"* A large number of Christians see the Christian community as a kind of totem pole—a hierarchy in which some Christians outrank others by virtue of their spectacular gifts or difficult place of service. For example, we may think of the pioneer missionary in some jungle village as being at the very top of the totem pole, with the well-known evangelist on the next notch down, and the ordinary church member or lay person in a lowly position at the bottom. Rather, Paul tells us that we are to see ourselves in relation to Christ and other Christians as members of a body. Jesus Christ is the head. Each member of the body—the hand or the foot, the eye or the ear—has a particular function. In a body, each part needs the other and the purpose of Christ will be fulfilled only as each finds and uses that gift.

But how do we discover our spiritual gifts? I am impressed with what Paul wrote to Timothy, one of his young helpers in the ministry of Christ. He told him *"to fan into flame the gift of God which is in you through the laying on of my hands"* (2 Tim. 1:6, NIV). That tells us three important things. Our spiritual gifts are initiated *by God*, mediated *through other* believers, and stimulated by our own faith and obedience. God takes the initiative in giving you a gift. He chooses to give you what he knows is best for you and best for his purposes. It is encouraging to know that God wants us to find fulfillment in using the gifts he has given us, not those he hasn't given us.

Then Paul told Timothy that his gift was received "through the laying on of my hands." That may indicate some kind of formal act of ordination but it also shows how spiritual gifts are mediated to us by other believers. Paul helped Timothy to find his gift and we too can go to some mature Christian and ask for counsel in identifying our gifts.

Paul also told Timothy "to stir into flame" the gift of God. In the winter I use a poker to stir up the dying embers in my fireplace. In the same way I need to stimulate the gift God has given to me. I need to study the Scriptures to know what the gifts are, to observe how other Christians use the gifts.

In my own experience, and that of many others, discovering spiritual gifts happens as we see another Christian exercising a particular gift and are drawn toward the same gift. As we experiment with, or exercise that gift, we will find that others are blessed and we ourselves are built up and fulfilled if, indeed, that is the gift that God has given to us.

That is the way it worked in my life. When I was in my mid-teens, through my contacts with the Youth for Christ movement, I met a number of gifted evangelists including Billy Graham. As I heard them preach and saw others come to Christ through their ministry, a flame was lit within me. I believed that God had given me that gift too.

The first evangelistic sermon I ever preached was at a little wooden church on the north shore of Lake Erie which was packed to the doors for a youth rally. I remember preaching on the dramatic scene recorded in the book of Daniel where the heathen king, Belshazzar, was having a wild feast and a hand wrote on the wall forecasting doom to Belshazzar's kingdom. In the flaming oratory of youth I talked about how Belshazzar's knees shook and a goblet dropped from his nervous fingers. At that precise moment someone dropped a hymn book and everybody in *the little wooden church jumped. (One of my friends who was there still believes that I deliberately had someone planted to drop the hymn book. I didn't, but I have never convinced him otherwise!)*

More important, that evening God drew a number of people to himself including a young Japanese Canadian girl of the Buddhist faith who encountered Jesus Christ as her Lord and Savior. He also touched a youthful farmer who has grown into a mature Christian in the years that have followed. It was a joy to discover one of my spiritual gifts, and to have God confirm it both by making this gift a blessing to others and by bringing a sense of fulfillment to my own life.

If you are still trying to find God's will don't expect it to come as you grit your teeth and seek to imitate some other Christian at the top of a totem pole whom you perceive to be more consecrated than yourself. And don't try to be a duck running on land. Instead, seek through the Bible and the counsel of other Christians and the leading of the Holy Spirit to identify your gift, and then to fan it into flame. As a result you should find fulfillment and growth in many other areas of your Christian experience.

Summer, 1967: Leighton Ford relaxes with his family.

LOVE, MARRIAGE, AND THE HOME

"A pastor must have only one wife. . . . He must enjoy having guests in his home. . . . He must have a well-behaved family with children who obey quickly and quietly" (1 Tim. 3:2, 4).

Dr. and Mrs. Leighton Ford at home.

8

JEAN COFFEY GRAHAM

Born in 1932 on her parents' dairy farm in Charlotte, the baby of the Graham family (after Billy, Catherine, and Melvin) enjoyed tagging along with her daddy down the furrows of his fields, into the dairy barn, and around the cow stanchions.

Jean was three when Mordecai Ham held his famed evangelistic campaign in Charlotte which turned the heart of her brother Billy toward God. William Franklin and Morrow Coffey Graham seldom left their farm because the cows had to be milked beginning at 2:30 each morning and the milk delivered to customers at dawn. One trip in 1935 took the family to Florida to visit Mrs. Graham's sister who owned a hotel. In the lobby, Billy lifted Jean up onto a table where she preached—with gestures just like Mordecai Ham—to the people passing by: "You are going to hell if you don't repent! Come to Jesus Christ." Billy was a Fuller Brush salesman at the time, so Jean had a head start on him as a preacher!

Jean learned to stack corn, to drive the horses pulling the hay wagon, and later to take a battered old Ford pickup over the fields on special errands.

The Carolinas in the forties teemed with infantile paralysis. At twelve, Jean was stricken with bulbar poliomyelitis which partially paralyzed her left side and her throat. Their physician knew nothing better than hospitalization. The hospital staff knew nothing better than to put Jean into a stiflingly hot tent erected on the lawn to accommodate the overflow of patients. She had to endure hot packs to make her perspire profusely twenty-four hours a day and to keep her feet against a wooden plank at the end of the cot.

Mr. Graham studied the situation and decided the no-exercise treatment was wrong. One morning when the three-week quarantine was over, he walked into the hospital and announced to the head nurse: "Miss Reinhardt, I've come to take my daughter home."

Before the shocked staff could protest, the tall, raw-boned farmer laid down a ten-dollar bill, picked up his baby girl and walked out.

He built a chinning bar so she could exercise while Mrs. Graham cooked soft food and set out cool, raw milk. Before the first meal was over Mrs. Graham was in tears because her daughter choked on every bite.

Jean was left with damaged, involuntary throat muscles that she must force to use when swallowing. Occasionally a weakness in her left side manifests itself but generally she enjoys good health.

When Jean was well again she returned to stacking corn, driving the horses, and commandeering the old pickup. At fourteen she learned to milk cows, but when she started going to school smelling like a barn her parents made her quit.

Jean assumed that she would attend Sharon High School as her two brothers and sister had, but since things were better financially her parents decided she should drive their old 1938 Plymouth to a city high school for a better education. Jean had little time left for study after driving so far each day but she was active in the youth group at Calvary Presbyterian Church. She "tended to be pious . . . didn't wear makeup . . . sat with girl friends at the dances without participating . . . never went to movies. . . ." She took these taboos to Bob Jones University in South Carolina for her freshman year and afterward to Wheaton College for the remaining three years.

During Jean's senior year at Wheaton Leighton sent

bright, clever letters with creative configurations from his seminary a thousand miles away. The sweethearts agreed not to use the word "love" until after they were betrothed. But they found other words to convey the timeless emotions which had to be expressed.

Jean appreciated the letters but the distance and the absence of stated intentions began whittling away at her confidence. She considered Leighton "awfully, awfully slow!" What *were* his plans about making their relationship permanent?

"I did what was a very stupid thing," she says as she looks back on her senior panic. "I told the Lord that if Leighton didn't propose by the end of 1952 I would know that our romance had died and that I should break off our relationship."

Leighton was invited to the Graham's nine-room farm house for the Christmas holidays. At 11:30 on New Year's Eve he and Jean were seated on an ornate living room sofa when Leighton began a lengthy tale about searching the world for the legendary "True Light." He had looked everywhere, he said with feigned anxiety, without success. At two minutes until midnight he announced, "I have finally found it. I found it in my true love's eyes!" He got down on his knees and asked Jean to marry him.

"I'd love to," she replied.

"Let's pray!" said Leighton. The clock struck midnight in the middle of his invocation. The year 1952 had ended. Jean's dreams had begun.

(Later he teased, "You said you'd *love* to marry me, but you didn't say you would.")

The ordeal may have taxed him beyond expectations because on the following day he succumbed to influenza and had to spend the holidays in bed at the Graham home before returning to school.

All during that Christmas holiday Mrs. Graham was secretly testing Leighton's theology. At appropriate times she asked, "What do you think about the inspiration of the Bible . . . about the deity of Jesus Christ . . . about the second coming?" When the holidays had ended she was satisfied that her future son-in-law was "a firm believer in the Lord and would rightly divide the Word of God." She believed that people in love are sometimes blinded and she took seriously her responsibility to make certain that Jean was marrying a genuine Christian.

Now that Leighton's quest for the "true light" had ended, what was the hurry to marry? He returned to seminary and plunged again into studies. "Jeanie" graduated from Wheaton in June 1953 and began planning for her wedding day. It was Leighton's intention to marry in the spring of 1954, but Billy had invited his sister to join the team for the historic Harringay Arena crusade in London that winter. Leighton learned that Donn Moomaw, a UCLA All-American football player, would also be joining the team.

"I didn't want Jeanie over there in that cold England winter with an All-American football hero," he says with a twinkle. So on December 19, 1953, most of the Graham team converged on the Calvary Presbyterian Church to help Leighton and Jean tie the knot.

While guests were being ushered into the candle-lit sanctuary, a singer traveling with John Wesley White, who was in the wedding, went to the piano and accompanied himself as he belted out the song, "It's Real" until he was stopped by an usher. All over the world he has since told people that he sang at Leighton and Jean Ford's wedding.

When Bev Shea began to sing "I Love Thee, Dear," Billy, who was to perform the ceremony, whispered backstage, "That's our cue."

"You're not going to wear those white gloves!" Grady Wilson exclaimed. "You won't be able to turn the pages or handle the rings."

Billy quickly slipped them off and stepped into the auditorium. But he had responded to the wrong cue and gone out too early. He had to stand there nodding and smiling to the guests through the preliminary music until it was time to officiate. He was never allowed to forget stumbling over the lines that came out: "Inasmuch as Leighton and Jean have exchanged wings . . . ah, that is, rings. . . ." There was so much comedy the bride wasn't altogether certain afterward that she was finally married.

After more than a quarter century of marriage, Leighton still leaves pillow notes for Jean to find after he's gone on a trip—sweet nothings, no directives. She tucks a note in his briefcase to be read when he unpacks.

On each of Leighton's numerous trips to Australia he (1) left a note on Jean's pillow, (2) mailed one in Los Angeles, and (3) mailed another from Honolulu. A note received during those first few days kept love keen and telescoped the time apart.

December 19, 1953: Leighton Ford and Jean Graham are married at Calvary Presbyterian Church in Charlotte, North Carolina. The best man, to Leighton's right, is the author, Norman Rohrer. Billy Graham is performing the ceremony. To Billy's left is Dr. L. P. McClenny, Jean's pastor. Ruth (Mrs. Billy Graham) is Jean's matron of honor.

IN LOVE: ARE FINDERS KEEPERS?

When my parents and I decided that Wheaton College would be a good place for me to study, we asked Billy Graham to write a letter of recommendation to the president. In it he mentioned his sister, Jean, whom he wanted to go to Wheaton in a future year. From that point on, every time I went on a date my mother would say, "Now you haven't met Billy Graham's sister yet." At the same time Billy had told Jeanie about meeting me in Canada and when she got to Wheaton he wanted her to look me up. Neither of us wanted to be pushed so we didn't get in touch.

I can remember the first time I saw Jeanie. She was sitting in the row ahead of me in chapel. She looked interesting, but I don't think I was overly impressed. She wasn't impressed at all when she first saw me! Then came the double date which John Wesley White arranged so I could meet Jeanie (which was a mean thing to do to the girl I was dating!). That night in the stadium an elderly lady who was a raucous Chicago Blackhawks fan cheered so loudly her teeth actually fell out!

After I got to know Jeanie, I was a little intimidated by her. She was a warm, outgoing, Southern girl and I was a shy, reserved Canadian. I finally got up my nerve and asked her for a date. To my amazement she accepted. That first date was a complete disaster. Why she ever accepted another invitation, I don't know, but she did. For some reason on that second date "it" happened . . . that intangible, wonderful, unexplainable, magnetic pull that the Bible calls "the way of a man with a maid."

What is that subtle, mysterious combination that draws a man and a woman to each other? Physical chemistry? Certainly Jeanie had that, as far as I was concerned, with her beautiful sparkling eyes, her golden hair, her lovely figure. Emotional need? I suppose that each of us has in our minds an *ideal picture of what is desirable in the person we want to marry. In Jeanie I saw gaiety, an outgoing, positive, warm personality, an unselfishness, a stability and security that, coming as I did from my family background, meant a great deal.*

And yet I suppose that for each of us there are many people who could ignite that spark in us. What is it that distinguishes love from infatuation? How can we know that we have found love?

I like to define love as a total commitment to the highest good of the other—the one I love. Love is giving, not getting. That's a basic difference between love and infatuation. Infatuation is self-centered while love is other-person centered. Infatuation says, "Meet my needs," while love says, "Let me meet your needs." Infatuation wonders whether she can make me happy; love wonders if I can make her happy. We may say, "I love you," but really mean, "I love me, and I want you." A basic question is whether I tend to use the other person for my needs or whether I care sincerely about that person's happiness. "Love does not demand its own way," says the Bible. To love like that we need to know and respond to the kind of love which Jesus Christ had for us.

Love is commitment to the other person, not just a feeling. We have been hoodwinked in our day to identify love with romantic emotions. Of course, love has feelings. When Jeanie and I fell in love we certainly didn't do it out of a cold sense of duty. But love is more than a feeling, more than something you "fall in." It's something you "stand in," something you do—a commitment.

That is the kind of love God had for us. He didn't simply look at a fallen, broken world and have pity. He "loved the world" so much that he gave his only Son" (John 3:16). That is the kind of love Jesus had. "He loved me and gave himself for me" said Paul.

Love is a total commitment which involves all of me, not just a part. It is physical, psychological, and spiritual. In this connection it is interesting to note that the New Testament has three words to express love. "Eros" has the connotation of sexual love while "phileia" has more the meaning of friendship. A third word, "agape," expresses God's kind of love, an unconditional self-giving commitment to another person. This transcends and outlasts chemistry and psychological need. It's a servant-love which is fully committed to the other.

Finding love is a bit like building a fire. The initial attraction is like the kindling which gets it going. The small sticks and logs we put on are like the growing friendship and commitment which gets the fire blazing. The "agape" love, God's servant kind of love, is like those big logs which can keep the fire burning through a long, cold night.

But in love, are finders keepers? Can that love keep burning? Before Jeanie and I got married we worried about this. We saw so many middle-aged people who had become cynical and would smile knowingly when we walked into a room holding hands as if to say, "You'll get over it." It is easy today to let other things breach that first commitment. Children or a job can come between. Commitment has been devalued in our age and marriage treated like a prison. By the time we get to middle age we have so many other commitments it becomes easy to take each other for granted.

A Philadelphia sociologist sent some grad students to live in homes and record conversation between married people. He found that the average couple spoke to each other a total of seven minutes a day and that included saying, "Please pass the salt!"

As with fire in a fireplace, love can die down. Then we can do one of two things. We can assume that love is an uncontrollable romantic passion that once gone, is gone. Or we can remember that God's kind of love is a commitment to the other person and like any commitment can be renewed. In Ephesians Paul speaks of love as an imperative. He tells husbands to "love their wives as Christ loved the church." Love includes attitudes and actions that can be willed and directed.

When the fire starts to die in our fireplace I take a poker, thrust it deep into the logs and make it flame up again. Jeanie and I had an experience like that not long ago. We loved each *other deeply, but yet we had come to take each other for granted. Our emotional fuel had become depleted as we poured ourselves out in other directions—helping other people in our ministry, going through Sandy's heart surgery, identifying with Debbie and her traumatic teenage years, taking care of Jeanie's mother in her physical needs, etc. We didn't pray together or read the Bible together as we had in the past. We had somehow come to accept each other in the roles that each of us had to fulfill. In deeper ways than ever before we needed each other physically, emotionally, and spiritually. Yet we didn't really open up and share and talk about these needs. Jeanie very deeply needed my affirmation as a woman and a wife. I had begun to experience the terrible loneliness of my traveling ministry.*

Then unexpectedly, God surprised us. We had gone on a vacation with the children, expecting just a time of recreation and rest. But God thrust a poker into the fire! Something broke through the shell we had come to accept around each other. We spoke honestly to each other. It was a deep and painful encounter, but a rediscovery of each other out of the depths of the love God had given to us.

I can remember walking on a beach and feeling utterly inadequate to meet Jeanie's needs and hardly knowing how to pray. I just prayed one word: "Love." And the next day in ways that were completely beyond what I could have done I was able to express love to Jeanie.

The following day I prayed just the single word, "Joy." I was able to find ways to bring a new kind of joy to her and the children. We fell in love again that week. Our kids hardly knew what had happened to mom and dad.

Can we find love in the superficiality of our age? Can our homes be "a haven in a heartless world?" Can that love stay alive? Or can it come alive again? We are convinced that we can and it can. But even our best-meaning human efforts at love are not enough. Only God can do it. Only God can give it.

9

HEARTHSIDE —
AN EARLY HEAVEN

If the Reverend Doctor Leighton Ford is anything he is a family man. His own growing up was so empty of associations with relatives that he tends to guard with perhaps exaggerated concern his time alone with wife and children. To an impatient member of his team who suggested to me that Leighton could do more if he were not so devoted to his family I say: The evidence that it pays off is on Leighton's side. If a man fails here he succeeds at nothing.

"The lines have fallen unto me in pleasant places," Leighton commented as we walked beneath the pines, water oaks, and dogwood surrounding his two-story home constructed with elegant old-brick in southern Charlotte.

A persistent rumor spreads the word that Leighton is wealthy, the recipient of a large legacy left him by affluent parents. Unfortunately, the rumor isn't true. Leighton's father died on February 28, 1962, six months before Jean's father passed away. Mr. Ford left only the wares of Ford's Jewellers whose auction yielded approximately $18,000. Mrs. Ford died in 1971, leaving no insurance policy, a collection of worthless furniture, and one large diamond ring which Leighton and Jean found wrapped in tissue paper and stuffed into the pocket of a discarded bathrobe. It became a gift for Jean to wear.

What about Jean's legacy? William Franklin Graham Sr. held the view that inheritances are left to sons; daughters were to be looked after by their husbands. Therefore, Billy and Melvin were named in his will; daughters Catherine and Jean would share in the sale of the old homestead when their mother passed away, besides whatever funds were left in the bank. The daughters were given a piece of property which they sold to provide funds for their children's education.

"I have to work for a living like other people," commented Leighton.

His salary is set by the BGEA executive committee. He keeps no honoraria from speaking engagements. Certain friends donate to BGEA each year funds designated for Leighton's crusades. Tithes and offerings from the Ford family exchequer are figured on a scale graduating upward: 10 percent to a certain amount; 12½ percent for the next amount; 15 percent for income above that.

Good books and time to read them are special enrichment at home. Approximately 2,500 volumes line Leighton's study walls. Has he read them all? "Some of them twice." Does he remember what's in them? "Select one and I'll try."

I pulled down an aging book written more than a generation ago by E. Stanley Jones titled, *Conversion*.

"In that book he explains how conversion takes place and uses various illustrations to clarify his remarks. He talks about the fact of the miracle of creation . . . the miracle of the birth of Jesus . . . and he discusses the creation of matter, the creation of mankind, the new creation in Jesus, the results of conversion. . . ."

A collection of novels adorns a separate shelf to furnish relaxation at night and to induce sleep. Espionage and politics are two of Leighton's favorite themes in fiction.

Travis, Green, Tournier, Neill, Speer, Gordon, Guinness—authors innumerable refresh his mind and provide subjects for sermons, radio talks, letters, writing, and counseling.

The books Leighton has written include: *The Christian Persuader* (Harper & Row), 1966; *One Way to Change the World* (Harper & Row), 1970; *Letters to a New Christian* (Worldwide Publications), 1966-67; *New Man, New*

World (Word), 1972; *Good News Is for Sharing* (Cook), 1977.

Dozens of his sermons which have become articles for periodicals are distributed continually by his team associates.

In 1962, Leighton was awarded the Doctor of Divinity Degree by Houghton College in Houghton, New York; in 1973 Gordon College in Wenham, Massachusetts, honored him with the Doctor of Laws degree. These are in addition to his Master of Divinity degree and his Bachelor of Arts degree from Columbia and Wheaton respectively.

Next to God comes Jeanie, then the children: Deborah Jean born in 1958; "Sandy" (Leighton Frederick Sandys Ford Jr.), born in 1960; and Kevin Graham, born in 1965. Close friends of the family observe that Leighton is more relaxed in social situations when Jean is with him. He consults her before making big decisions. When anger interrupts their continuing romance it is usually Leighton who first says he's sorry. On the other hand, Jean is probably more sensitive to his needs than he is to hers. Leighton is oriented to thought, Jean to practicality. Leighton reads books, Jean reads books and people. Leighton drives his Olds Cutlass, Jean notices when the tires are worn out.

Leighton is away from home 45 percent of his working hours. Jean still cries when she takes him to Charlotte's Douglas Airport for another flight. But when she gets a case of "poor-me," she tries to turn that energy into praying for Leighton. He's the one who has to go into that cold, lonely hotel room at night, she reminds herself.

Jean decorates with Early American and tasteful traditional styles, cooks simply, and appreciates Leighton's help cleaning up except that "he never gets the corners." Both are thrifty and seldom buy on impulse. Jean makes decisions quickly, Leighton deliberates sometimes to the point of exasperating his wife. Jean's worst outburst of temper came when Leighton once compared her handling of the children to that of his mother's.

"You and Dad have such a good marriage you don't have to work at it, do you, Mom?" Sandy asked one day.

"Yes, we do, son," Jean replied, "yes, we do."

'DEBBIE JEAN'

"Baby," as she was called by her proud father all through her teens, sat primly—the picture of health and charm—on a sofa at Williston Hall on Wheaton's campus, a few feet from where her parents had first met.

"I love being with dad," she told me. "He lets me know he is proud of me. He is never critical and if he suggests a change he does it in a loving way."

For years, Leighton told Debbie bedtime stories about the "House with the Golden Windows." To avoid the tedium of a twice-told tale, he varied the plot every night.

Debbie was seven when she heard her father preach on the steps outside Sharon Presbyterian Church and made a commitment to Jesus Christ. That early decision was renewed at thirteen, a turning point in the life of this strong-willed young lady.

Debbie usually self-disclosed late at night, or on Sunday afternoons. Her mother remembers the "hours and hours" listening to her eldest child talk through her problems, and the "miles and miles" walking the street to get a matter settled. Debbie's appraisal of her self is that she is somewhat spoiled ("Mom had a maid three mornings a week and I rarely did any housework"), and independent ("I tend to be opinionated and stick to my view unless I'm otherwise convinced").

Debbie was spanked and strongly disciplined. All through her senior year at high school she obeyed an 11:30 curfew, and knows what it feels like to have her mouth washed out with soap. Looking back, Leighton admits to occasionally losing his temper with the ones he loves most. He has often had to apologize, realizing he acted too quickly or punished them too severely. "Yet, I think our children have sometimes asked for discipline. They seemed to be crying out, saying: 'Pay attention to me!' And after the punishment things were always better."

Debbie was always complimented when her father would invite her on a walk when she arrived home from school. On those walks he would often show her his notes for a message to youth and ask for her opinion. Just as often she would tell him how she thought her generation would react, and Leighton would modify his remarks accordingly.

Debbie Jean—attractive, bright, easy to meet. Surely of all people she "has it all together," yet her strong personality and tendency to dominate mask what her mother calls a sensitive personality. A striving for perfection gets in the way of good self-esteem: she is an excellent pianist, but wanted to be a prodigy; she is an A student but wanted to be brilliant; she is well coordinated for sports but would have preferred to be a world class tennis player. Debbie is now engaged in graduate studies in speech communication at the University of North Carolina.

She is "extremely motivated and goal-oriented," and has "a hard time figuring out my place as a woman *i.e.* career vs. housewife, or both. The only thing that makes me totally happy and secure is thinking of the Lord and seeing him use me to further his kingdom. My marriage, my goals, my thoughts must be totally his, and focused on my number one goal of serving Jesus Christ."

SANDY

The Fords' goal-oriented, self-motivated, perfectionist first-born son is a kid everyone likes. He stands straight, excels in sports, pulls top grades, speaks respectfully. . . .

Sandy has no yellow light. It's always green. When he plays too hard, stays up too late, or teases Kevin too much Leighton warns, "Bud, put the yellow light on."

Sandy traces his conversion to age six when he watched a TV special on which his Uncle Billy preached.

"Do I have to be there to do that?" he asked as people moved forward in response to Billy's message on the Ten Commandments.

At thirteen he made a public decision for Christ in a church service following a fight with his brother about which he felt remorseful.

In 1577 an English poet-minister named Sandys told his friends: "I have taught you, my dear flock, for above thirty years how to live; and I will show you in a very short time how to die." Nearly two centuries later his namesake, Sandys Ford, five weeks before his fifteenth birthday, had to face the possibility that it might be within God's permissive will for him also to die.

After a vigorous basketball game on October 7, 1975, his heart began to race. Weakly, Sandy phoned home, and by the time Jean picked him up and got him to a doctor his heart was beating four to five times the normal rate. Leighton was finishing supper in New York, preparing to address a group of Methodist ministers at the Thomas Watson camp grounds when the news came. He was able to get a plane home that same evening, but by then the doctors had the heartbeat slowed and Sandy was resting normally.

The boy had taken treatment for tachyarrhythmias associated with Wolff-Parkinson-White syndrome. Sandy had been born with an extra electrical pathway in his heart where only one is needed to keep the beat regular. It is a muscular bundle which transmits an electrical signal, causing the heart to function. Getting Sandy's paroxysmal tachycardia under control was, Dr. Blair Bryan said, "10 percent drugs and 90 percent prayer." A specialist said Sandy "could live a lifetime without a recurrence or he could die tomorrow."

Fleeces which the Fords laid before the Lord all pointed to corrective surgery. Leighton phoned several medical specialists and all leads pointed to Duke University one hundred and twenty-five miles north at Durham. Dr. John J. Gallagher, the electro-physiological cardiologist, and Dr. Will C. Sealy, the cardiac surgeon, answered Sandy's questions slowly and deliberately.

When the date was set Sandy was frightened. He asked a lot of general questions, his eyes wide with apprehension. He cried. He asked God, "Why me?" and then he began asking intelligent, specific questions. Leighton and Jean saw their son "grow up" in the space of three hours. Sandy accepted the fact that on the following Monday morning his chest would be sawn open, his heart exposed in an operation that, as far as they knew at that time, offered him only a fifty-fifty chance of a complete cure. While Sandy prepared himself for the knife, his parents put their emotions in order so they could walk with him through his suffering.

On Monday morning, November 10, 1975, Sandy closed his eyes beneath the sterile sheets in the operating room. Bill Bright, president of Campus Crusade for Christ, and his wife rose at 4 A.M. to pray for Sandy. The office staffs of the Billy Graham Evangelistic Association in Minneapolis, Atlanta, and around the world formed a chain of intercession. People the Fords had never met in Australia, Europe, South America, and Asia prayed too. Pat Robertson on the daily TV "700 Club" broadcast from Portsmouth called his TV listeners to prayer for Sandy Ford.

The surgical procedure for interruption of the Kent bundle consists of two steps: the first is identification of the pathway and the second is its interruption. Dr. Sealy exposed the heart through a median sternotomy and monitored the impulses of the heart. He cut the front circuit but the trouble wasn't there. He lifted the heart out and put his probe in the rear of the organ, closer . . . closer . . . closer to the pathway circuit which would show on his monitor in this, only the forty-seventh operation of its kind at Duke.

Outside Leighton paced the dreary corridors of Duke. *Lord, you were Sandy's father before I was. He's your son before he is mine. Lord, he is yours whether it's life or whether it's death.*

Dr. Sealy probed until he found and cut the errant pathway. He thrust his delicate rapier to within one millimeter of the normal conductor system. He cut, and it was a success.

He waited for the usual trauma but all systems were steady. He left the heart outside Sandy's chest for one hour to make certain all bleeding had stopped. He took Sandy off the heart-lung machine and watched for the usual fluttering. None. He watched for a drop in blood pressure—nothing unusual. Associates closed the wound and wired Sandy's rib cage shut. His strong heart beat normally again. It was over.

Through eyes wet with tears Leighton read to Jean and Debbie and Kevin Hosea 6:1, 2:

> Come, let us return to the Lord; it is he who has torn us—he will heal us. He has wounded—he will bind us up. In . . . three [days] at the most, he will set us on our feet again, to live in his kindness! Oh, that we might know the Lord! Let us press on to know him, and he will respond to us as surely as the coming of dawn or the rain of early spring.

People seemed to observe Leighton differently after that. The Ford family's pastor, Ross Rhoads, said: "I've watched a lot of people under stress. Even though Leighton was deeply moved, fully aware of his son's suffering and possible death, he didn't crack. He had no facade to come off when the pressure mounted. His faith was strong. The roots were there."

Others saw him not only as a speaker on a platform but as a father who could weep, who needed help. Through it all God was saying, "Look, I'm in control." God was surprising the Fords, showing them that he really is God. He knew Leighton's problem about needing to be in control, his perfectionism, his impatience when things went wrong. . . .

Leighton thanked his associates at a Billy Graham team meeting two months later in January 1976 at Orlando: "Many of you without realizing it have ministered to Jeanie and myself," he began. "In an experience such as we've been through you cannot help reassessing what your life is about . . . what your priorities are."

Sandy, now a student at the University of North Carolina, told me he didn't think a book about his father would be complete without showing his relationship with his children.

"He is one of those fathers that you can say, 'I would like to grow up to be like him,' " Sandy wrote. "He spends so much of his time working, yet he always seems to have time for us. He probably does the work of two average men but still finds time. . . . A lot of people think I might end up a minister, like dad. Who knows? I might. But my dad has never put pressure on me whatsoever. He just hopes that I might pursue God's will, whatever it may be. It could be a minister, a doctor, a lawyer, a business man, or a mountain climber; but like him, I think it should be God's will."

One winter evening after Leighton had coached a team in Charlotte's YMCA basketball league in which Sandy had played a hard-fought game he penned this poem for his son:

COACH

He jumped
higher than at the basket

faster than the ball had bounced
into my arms.
My son had won
another game.

And in that momentary hard embrace
a celebration passed between us
bigger than winning.
I will not always be there, Lord,
but You will.

Help me teach him
in winning joy
or losing pain
always to leap . . .
straight . . .
into Your arms.

KEVIN GRAHAM FORD

While Sandy is the intense, goal-oriented achiever,
Kevin is the guy who enjoys staying at home with his
family, his friends, and his books. He and Leighton have
read through the seven-volume *Chronicles of Narnia* series
together at bedtime, and Kevin has read the first one, *The
Lion, the Witch and the Wardrobe* half a dozen times by
himself.

On Kevin's thirteenth birthday Leighton asked him to
pray that night at the dinner table. His prayer showed a
positive self-image: "Thank you for Mom, thank you for
Dad, thank you for Debbie, thank you for Sandy, and
thank you for even me."

Kevin possesses astonishing powers of recall. Ask him
about people, places, and things he's heard in the news,
whom he played with five years ago on Christmas Day,
what color his trousers were on that date, and what they
had for dinner. You'll get an instant replay.

Kevin plays first trumpet in his band and he is first

string forward on his basketball team.

He wanted to write a tribute to his dad. With pencil and yellow note pad, this lad (then twelve) spoke from the heart:

Dear Mr. Rohrer:

I think Dad is super! I mean most dads are too busy to play with their kids but Dad always takes time to stop his work and play with me. I think it's great to have a father like mine!

Some of the happiest times I can think of with Dad was riding to Cheeseman Lake, on horseback, in Lost Valley Ranch, Colorado; rockhopping in the Franklin River in Highlands, N.C., and walking down Glenn Falls with him. I also liked reading the books of Narnia by C. S. Lewis. I have a great time throwing the football and shooting baskets with him. But to top it all, Dad's a Christian! I love, respect, and enjoy him!

> Sincerely,
> Kevin Ford.

One evening Leighton and then six-year-old Kevin ran across Sharon Road into South Park shopping center to order a pie. As Leighton watched the baking process he suddenly realized his little son wasn't tall enough to take in the action. Leighton knelt beside him, then lifted him up. Later he penned a bit of verse which went into their Christmas card to family friends:

DOWN

I knelt one time
beside my six-year son
to see how big things looked
from where he stood.
"It sure looks big down here,"
I said.
He smiled.

God knelt down too,
one Christmas,
to wipe away sin's stains
and make us smile again.

WHAT MY CHILDREN HAVE TAUGHT ME

Fred Rogers of "Mr. Rogers' Neighborhood" fame, believes that Jesus learned a lot from children. As I look back over our family life, we can see much that our children have taught us.

Our three children now cover the span from early through late adolescence. Debbie is now involved in graduate study and looking forward to a career in the area of communications. Sandy, our oldest boy, is at the University of North Carolina and we still have our youngest, Kevin, to see through the ups and downs of high school years!

Debbie was born on a Sunday morning in 1958, just shortly before I had to preach at a local church. Between services I rushed to the hospital and all I could think of that morning was the "new birth!" When I got my first glimpse of her through the plate glass of the hospital nursery I thought, "That's over!" And then suddenly it hit me, "No, it's just begun." Later when our two boys were born, Jeanie and I felt again the weight of responsibility of parenthood, knowing how much there was to teach them. But the surprise that God had in store for us was that we would learn just as much from them as they ever learned from us.

Like most parents today, Jeanie and I feel a sense of anxiety as we see our children going out to live their lives in what often seems like a moral wilderness. Youth today are more vulnerable than ever.

Princeton University Professor Paul Ramsey says that far from living in a permissive society, we actually live in one of the most insistent societies there has ever been—insistent that our children give in to peer pressures, become sexually active, experiment with drugs. As my friend Fred Smith likes to say, "In the older generation when we got off the straight and narrow into the woods, we at least had a compass that showed us the way back; but today we have gotten our kids out in the woods and told them there is no compass." No wonder so many young people have been sucked in by the pseudo-religions and false cults of our day.

I know of no sure way of making young people walk the straight and narrow path but I do know that God's Word has some encouragements for parenting. "Teach a child to choose the right path and when he is older he will remain upon it," said King Solomon in this Proverb (which should probably be taken more as a general observation than as an invariable proposition). The Apostle Paul said to a jailer, "Believe on the Lord Jesus and you will be saved, and your entire household."

On a recent family outing, Jeanie and I asked our three children what had helped them the most in their own commitment to Christ and spiritual growth. Debbie, Sandy, and Kevin are not perfect. Like their parents they are unfinished stories, Christians under construction. But each has shown genuine evidence that God is at work in their lives. We think what they told us is worth passing on.

Kevin, our early teenager, was the first to speak and he had a surprising thing to say! "I think it is important that you have some rules," he said. "I don't always like them, but I know that I need them and they help me."

Debbie and Sandy agreed. In fact, Deb once told me that she wished that as her father I had been more strict than I was, that she knew she needed it and that discipline gave her a real feeling of security. Traveling as much as I have, I probably have left too much of Deb's discipline to Jeanie. If I were doing it again, I wouldn't be harsher, but I would be more firm with Deb. I think she needed to see this in her father more than she did.

Deb was next to speak. She said that probably the most important factor in her spiritual growth had been her friends, particularly in Young Life meetings which she attended regularly in high school. Kevin seconded this. He felt that experiences he had had at camp and the Christian friends and counselors he had met there had been a key factor with him.

What about church? Church attendance has not been a question mark with us but a normal expectation for Sundays. Occasional exceptions have been when we have had family worship on vacation. The church youth group has been a regular activity for the kids on Sunday nights.

Deb was honest in her response to this question. She felt the church had not, up to this point, been a central ingredient in her Christian commitment but that even so the habit was one that she needed to develop.

Kevin spoke particularly of the junior high group and the influence of the junior high group leaders who this past year had had fun with him and the others. They had trusted them, encouraged them to take leadership, to pray, and to relate their Christian faith to the practical experiences they were facing.

For Sandy, his church experience had been a very important factor. He appreciated camp and Young Life but the senior high youth group to which he had given leadership had been a vital factor in his experience.

Jeanie and I have come to believe that it is tremendously important to expose our children to Christian fellowship — particularly to an alive, Christ-centered fellowship. If the church which they attend is not alive and exciting then we would advise: seek to encourage change — or if change can't take place then we would perhaps even go so far as to advocate moving to another congregation.

At one point our children were at a church that was simply boring and stiff. After several years there was no sign of change. Jeanie and I might have ridden it out but our kids couldn't. We are glad that we made a switch to a church which was really alive and could hold their interest and challenge them with teaching from the Bible and a Christ-centered program. If you can't find a church like that in the area where you live, then send them to a Christ-centered Christian camp. It is worth whatever time, cost, and effort it takes to find one and whatever sacrifice it takes to get them there. This was true in my own life as a young person and I believe it has been true for our children.

What about the place the Bible has had in our home? All

three agreed that times for family Bible reading after meals in the evening had been important. Deb said she was glad that this wasn't something that was so rigid that it became just a habit.

Another thing that our children have taught us is that Bible reading and Bible discussion is not something for just a set time of devotions or Sunday morning in church. It is something that needs to be related to every part of our lives. In the Old Testament God told his people to love him and to impress his commandments on their children. "Talk about them when you are at home or out for a walk; at bedtime and the first thing in the morning," he said. "Write them on the doorposts of your house" (Deut. 6:7-9). We have tried to see that our children were exposed to the Word of God—in Sunday school and church, in family devotions. We have also found that some of the most effective times for teaching the Word of God are those special moments of childhood crisis. A fight between two siblings, a disappointment in a school election, a time of sickness, a broken romance—all of these are opportune moments to share at a deep level. Hearts are more open then to the strengthening and comforting truth of the Bible. We believe that children ought to get to know the Bible as the continuing story of what God is doing in our world and in our lives. This, we've found, is most effective when the Bible is grasped as a story—one long, true story. In fact, we found that it helped to have the children act out dramatic incidents—like Daniel in the lion's den. They really get inside them when they themselves become the actors and actresses!

Visitors in our home have been an important part of our family life. Jeanie believes in the grace of hospitality and our guest room has often been full. We asked the children whether having distinguished (or ordinary) Christians in the home for a meal or overnight had impressed them. Again, they were honest. They felt that because of my work, they weren't overly impressed with some "name" visitor. But Sandy spoke up quickly to say how grateful he was for Cliffe Knechtle, a basketball player and student leader at nearby Davidson College who stayed with us on many weekends. Cliffe became almost like a son to our family. His openness, his integrity, his courtesy and helpfulness, and *above all his strong commitment to Jesus Christ made a deep impression on our children—especially on Sandy—that we can still see and will never forget. We opened our home to Cliffe to help him but God surprised us by giving more back from our guest to our own children.*

Sandy brought the discussion to a close. "Of course," he said, "Mom and Dad have been the greatest influence."

How pleased we were. But of course we have no formula to develop godly children. Only God can produce his character in them, as only God can produce his likeness in us.

What parental advice we have learned from our children would go like this:

—show them the way, don't just tell them.

—teach them the Word.

—expose them to genuine Christian fellowship.

—keep the rules simple, but be firm.

—be available when they need you and on their schedule.

—keep open house.

—when the time comes, let them go and trust them to the Lord.

Leighton Ford doing a TV spot for the one-minute "Leighton Ford TV Feature."

THE WITNESS

"Bring others to Christ. Leave nothing undone that you ought to do" (2 Tim. 4:5).

1973: The Leighton Ford platform team: (from left to right) Irv Chambers, Leighton Ford, John Innes, Homer James.

10

THE
LEIGHTON FORD CRUSADES

When Leighton sailed for Great Britain in 1955 he sensed
that a momentous tide was cresting and he was determined to ride that crest into the work for which he felt he
had been born. What he had learned in books was now to
be translated into experience. Nothing could have dis-
suaded him from joining Billy.

During a stopover with the Graham team in London,
at Wembley Stadium, Leighton set to work preparing for
his first scheduled area-wide crusade in Falkirk, Scotland.
No materials had been prepared to guide the planners for
Falkirk so Leighton sat down at a typewriter and pecked
out the manuals for counselors, ushers, and committee
personnel. These materials, written when he was
twenty-three, were developed into procedures still being
used in the Leighton Ford Crusades.

For four Sundays he preached in historic old Wellington Church near the University of Glasgow. Later he
traveled north to the Scottish Highland cities of Buckie,
Banff, Tain, Nairn, Aberdeen, and then to the seacoast
towns of Gervin and Ayr. Only forty kilometers east of
Falkirk stood celebrated New College of Edinburgh
where Leighton sought the counsel of Professor James
Stewart concerning the possibilities for studies leading to
a doctorate. His mother had offered to pay all expenses.
Billy supported the move because, he said, "the world
needs evangelists with a Ph.D."

But the August 1955 Billy Graham Toronto crusade
loomed. Leighton decided to remain in the maelstrom.
Billy offered him seventy-five dollars a week to work in
Toronto and the status of Associate Evangelist. The pull

of the podium was too strong. The carrels at New College would have to wait.

The Toronto effort brought the Graham team back to North America in late summer that year and soon Leighton was busily preaching as an associate evangelist in the city of his birth. Toward the end of that two-week meeting a coterie of Ontario clergymen invited their countryman to hold small church crusades throughout the province. Leighton accepted their overtures and assembled a pick-up team. His first crusade in North America had been the 1953 week-long series of meetings at the Annie Linley Presbyterian Church in Anderson, South Carolina, where Jack Ward led the singing, Bill Herzog played the piano, Homer James sang, and Leighton preached. Newspaper ads had cried: "Save on your electric bill. Turn off your lights and come hear Leighton Ford preach!"

For the 1955 Ontario series he invited Homer James and later Irvine Chambers to join him. Homer was a dairy farmer living in Stittsville, Ontario, (near Ottawa) who had earned Dominion-wide acclaim after winning the CBC's "Talent Caravan Contest" by singing hymns on television with his dramatic tenor voice.

Irv was the youthful director of the Sacandaga Bible Conference in New York. Irv played the trumpet, entertained youth with magic, and was accustomed to taking charge of a platform. This loyal associate began as songleader, became a youth worker, and finally executive director of the Leighton Ford Crusades.

Homer, Leighton, Jean, and eventually Irv, worked their way through the provincial cities of Wingham, Arthur, Simcoe, Whitby, Oshawa, Tillsonburg, Orillia and Stratford. Often a supporter would lend them an empty house where Jean cooked and laundered for the team. Sometimes they would be guests of Christians in homes grand and humble, clean and marginal, near and far.

A host pastor in Arthur, Ontario, liked to awaken

them with a funeral dirge which he pounded out on the piano. Once when the electrical power was scheduled to be cut off from 6 to 7:30 A.M. he called the team members at 5:30 rather than letting them sleep until 7:30.

In another rural home near Arthur, Ontario, Homer, Leighton, and Jean were invited to dinner by a mentally retarded hostess who had two retarded daughters and a husband in jail. She had nothing prepared when they walked to the front door through a sea of mud. She eventually served some poorly cooked food on dishes rimmed with dirt.

"It was awfully nice of you to invite us," Leighton said, selecting a piece of bread. "But I don't really eat much before I speak."

"And I don't eat much before I sing," Homer apologized.

They all looked at Jeanie. "Actually, I don't eat much before Leighton speaks," she said.

In 1956 Leighton and Jean moved to an apartment on New York's Twenty-third Street to direct church relations in preparation for the historic 1957 Billy Graham Greater New York Crusade. Leighton traveled the vast target area, talked to ministers, preached in churches of Manhattan, the Bronx, Brooklyn, Staten Island, Long Island, North Jersey, Westchester County, and Queens. He created a kind of control center and took full charge of booking the associate evangelists during the united effort—men like Paul Rees, Joe Blinco, Tom Allan, Stephen Olford and many others.

"Leighton made a mistake and allowed me five minutes without a meeting today," Howard Butt of Texas joked.

The New York Crusade opened May 15, 1957, ran for 16 weeks, and registered a total attendance of 2,397,400 in Madison Square Garden.

When the calendar turned down 1958 Leighton responded to invitations from Jamaica and other Caribbean ports throughout the month of January. He would preach in one city for a week then Billy would arrive to conduct the final mass rally.

In Kingston, Leighton addressed 15,000 Jamaicans, the largest audience of his crusades to date. Many were simple folk who responded to the preaching with emotional gusto.

"Your body may be alive, but your soul is dead."

"O-o-o-o-oh!" the audience would moan.

"In ten years 25 percent of this audience will be dead."

"Amen!" cried an illiterate fellow, not quite hearing what had been said.

Grand old Anglican Canon R.O.C. King had to instruct his people more perfectly. He began opening each meeting with a call for more robust singing and loud praise. Then he would tell them, "Now it is time to be quiet while Mr. Ford preaches."

The itinerary led from banana wharfs to stately cathedrals. Leighton's outdoor audiences would be regularly drenched by fickle showers, but the Jamaicans seemed not to mind.

During his final meeting en route home in Panama City he placed a complicated long-distance overseas call and learned that Deborah Jean was on the way. Jean was staying with her parents and when the overseas operator first rang the farm Mr. Graham took the call. He listened a moment and hung up.

"Who was it?" Jean asked.

"Oh, just some crazy woman mumbling something in Spanish about Panama."

Leighton started the whole procedure over again and Jean sat near the phone to tell him the good news that she was expecting their first child.

Leighton's Canadian citizenship added to his appeal in the Commonwealth countries of Australia and New Zealand where he joined the 1959 Billy Graham Sydney Crusade. In Brisbane he preached to crowds numbering up to 20,000. In Wellington, New Zealand, he felt the icy winds blowing unhindered from the Antarctic. Each memorable detail of the five-month preaching tour was recorded in memos to Jean. In later years he dictated these memos to his secretary to share with his wife and an inner circle of friends and supporters.

"I won't allow myself to be away from home that long again," he commented. "Debbie Jean was a colicky baby who cried most of the time. It took Jeanie several years to completely get over that emotionally trying experience."

In 1962, following the Chicago crusade, Billy invited Leighton to his home in Montreat to discuss the future. "I think it's time you had a team of your own on a full-time basis," Billy suggested. "The association will back you financially. Concentrate on Canada if you like."

Leighton drove back over the 120 miles from Montreat to Charlotte with a new vision and a new task. He didn't know it then, but most of the men and women who would join the Ford team had already been introduced to him. It was now a matter of finding whom the Lord had ordained.

While sipping iced tea at his home with Irv and Bob Glockner, a former Navigator staff member who had joined Leighton temporarily for counselor training, Leighton remembered Australian Norman Pell—the young Baptist minister who had served on the committee for Billy's 1959 crusade meetings and had helped set up 1961 meetings for Leighton when he returned to Melbourne in the state of Victoria.

"Was Norman as good as he seemed? Or did he stand out because he so perfectly filled the bill for our meetings?" Leighton wondered.

In 1963 Norman left his responsibilities as director of evangelism for the Baptist Union in Australia, brought his wife Dorothy to North America, and joined Leighton. The Aussie possessed an indomitable spirit of enthusiasm, a flair for organization, and a gift for mobilizing clergymen. Team members soon learned that energetic Norman Pell's initiatives during a crusade proved to be workable and strategic. He blitzed committee members with directives, demanding of himself what he asked them to do. When the memos began to fly the staff knew: "Norman has had a think on."

Norman's motto was, "If we aren't worn out before the crusade begins we haven't done our job; and if Leighton doesn't arrive fresh and rested for his preaching *he* hasn't done *his* job."

A volunteer pianist in a small Australian town whom the team nicknamed "Knuckles" unwittingly accelerated the men's efforts to find a permanent and qualified pianist. John Innes joined them in 1962 following the Billy Graham Chicago Crusade.

John had felt the call to evangelism in his home at Bradford, England, when the sounds of Tedd Smith's piano at Harringay moved him as he listened to the Graham Crusade relayed by a land-line circuit in 1954. John later studied at Moody Bible Institute in Chicago, was enrolled at Wheaton College's conservatory of music, and later received his Master's Degree from Northwestern University. He joined Leighton as a permanent staff member in 1965.

During Billy's 1955 Toronto crusade Leighton met Stan Izon, president of Koinonia, an Anglican youth fellowship and an account executive with the prestigious advertising agency Kenyon and Eckhardt. In 1964 Stan brought a team of laymen to join Leighton's crusade in Halifax. One evening en route to the auditorium Leighton spotted Stan walking, rolled down the car window and called, "When are you coming with us?"

"When are you going to ask me?" Stan shot back.

He left his lucrative career on Good Friday of 1965 and joined Leighton's Vancouver Crusade on Easter Sunday. "It was my death and resurrection," says Stan.

He serves as director of advertising and information for the Ford crusades.

In the 1965 Vancouver crusade Ruth Love offered voluntary secretarial help and afterward left an insurance agency to become a permanent staff member. She is based at the Team Office in Minneapolis.

In 1968 Leola Linkous of Knoxville, Tennessee, became Leighton's personal secretary. She had come to the Lord through Lane Adams' ministry there. Leola lives only a few minutes by car from the Ford residence in Charlotte where she maintains an office in her own home, processes the mail, types Leighton's dictation, and files accumulated records.

Men such as Lane Adams, Calvin Thielman, Ben Haden, Melvin Graham, and the late Joe Blinco have joined the Ford team at various times for specific assignments. Other people who have been involved in the team as associate evangelists have been the late Paul Little, Akbar Haqq, and Ralph Bell of the Billy Graham team, David Hubbard, and Victor Nelson. Dr. Nelson, a former Presbyterian minister, was Leighton's first set-up man.

None has been more supportive of Leighton than the man most closely associated with Billy—Cliff Barrows. Both Cliff and Leighton give priority to responsibilities at home. They have trekked the hills and valleys of scenic places together with their families on many occasions.

To Cliff, Leighton has been "a very warm, wonderful team member whose genuine concern for people and sensitivity to situations have always been an inspiration and a challenge to us who know him."

From 1963 to 1968 Leighton concentrated his evangelistic efforts in thirty-five cities of Canada. The Atlantic Provinces first felt the impact of the team. Leighton arranged for Billy to preach at the closing rally in Halifax. Billy came a day early and slipped into the back of the stadium where he noticed a man who seemed to be under conviction as Leighton preached. At the invitation Billy offered to go forward with him if he wanted to make a decision.

The man didn't recognize Billy. He looked at the evangelist carefully and shook his head. "No, thanks. I think I'll wait for the big gun tomorrow night."

Leighton and each team member are paid according to salaries established by the BGEA board of directors. All money Leighton receives for speaking is turned into the Graham Association office in Minneapolis. He does not get a cut or a percentage or a salary from his crusades.

Crusade budgets involve only the local committee in whatever city is hosting the meetings. When this budget is prepared, the Billy Graham Evangelistic Association provides staff members to help in the organization. A portion of the salary of every staff member is written into the budget of the local crusade except for Leighton, who receives nothing. A contribution from the local crusade budget is made to BGEA at the close of the meeting series. This money is usually earmarked for the radio and television ministries of BGEA.

"The association assumes responsibility for financing our team operations and crusades and our team accepts the responsibility for raising through our crusades and through interested friends as much of the cost as possible throughout the year," Leighton explains.

Leighton selected the term "Reachout" for his crusades after noticing Debbie Jean reading her teen-age version of *The Living Bible* with that title. They tried it in the highly successful April 28—May 7, 1972, Rochester, New York meeting. The term is used interchangeably with "crusade," to meet the needs of each situation. Another title, used for example in the affluent North Shore of Chicago, was the "Festival of Faith."

Another dimension of "Reachout" is undertaken by Christian laymen who pay their own way and take preaching assignments throughout the crusade's metropolitan area. A committee member was amazed when twenty laymen suddenly appeared one day and asked to be put to work.

"Leighton Ford and his team are paid to be good, but you fellows are good for nothing," he teased.

The lay teams have been directed by Bob Foster of Colorado, and more recently by Ford Madison of Dallas. The visitors are invited to speak at service clubs; they are interviewed on radio; they conduct evening afterglows in homes; they address businessmen; they lead early-bird breakfasts which often grow from a handful of men to a couple of hundred.

In a Huntsville, Alabama, hotel lobby a news reporter asked Leighton, "Do the converts in your crusades last?"

Leighton spotted Chuck McGowan, a physician from Youngstown, Ohio, and called him over. "Chuck, this lady wants to know if converts last. Now, you were an inquirer at an evangelistic crusade. Was your life changed?"

"No," he replied.

Oh, my goodness, I've asked the wrong guy! Leighton gasped mentally.

"No," Chuck continued, "I wasn't *changed,* because spiritually I wasn't even alive. I was dead. I am a totally new person because of what God did for me at a crusade like this."

When people ask "Why city-wide crusades?" the Ford team answers, "Why not?" for the following reasons:

1. An evangelistic crusade makes an impact on a city. As Christian people work together, media take notice. There is access to television, radio, and newspapers which doesn't last forever but which generates publicity for weeks and even months. It creates an atmosphere for talking about faith. People seek answers to their questions openly.

2. An evangelistic crusade is a launching pad for community penetration into high schools, college campuses, service clubs, homes, factories—wherever the team can go to reach people not ordinarily touched.

3. An evangelistic crusade reaps where others have

sown. Gospel seed sown faithfully day after day for years in a community often is reaped in conversions during the concentrated effort of a crusade.

4. An evangelistic crusade fosters neighborhood Bible studies. Christian people united in a gospel outreach often continue those efforts in their own districts after the crusade has ended.

5. An evangelistic crusade has a catalytic effect. Knowing that the event is coming, Christians are quickened to make an all-out Christian witness. They train workers, equip churches for follow-up, and provide funds that otherwise would not be available for evangelism.

6. An evangelistic crusade unites Christians for a common task. This is seen as the greatest value of their efforts. Pastors learn to trust each other. Christians exclaim, "I didn't know there were so many believers at my school until the crusade began."

Two types of Christians are suspicious of a crusade effort. One is the ultra-conservative who feels that the meeting compromises the gospel by associating with people of liberal views; the other type is the ultra-liberal who doesn't believe in the authority of the Scriptures and looks upon such preaching as simplistic, shallow, and disruptive.

"We welcome to partnership anybody who is in agreement with the message we preach, which is the gospel," Leighton declares. "Anybody who doesn't agree with that and who has the integrity to say so needs to rule himself out. Anybody is welcomed who agrees with the New Testament message that Jesus Christ was God come in the flesh . . . that God was in Christ reconciling the world unto himself . . . that Christ died for our sins according to the Scriptures, that he was buried and rose again the third day according to the Scriptures . . . that we are saved by grace through faith not of ourselves, it is the gift of God—not of works, although we are saved *unto* good works and to a life of service and love. Anybody who believes in those basics of the gospel is welcomed to participate."

Often the problem is not the content of the message but the unwillingness of some to work with those who are not of their own group. This premise is weakened, members of the Ford team believe, by Jesus' words against the disciples who rejected a man because he cast out demons in Jesus' name but wasn't among their band: "He who is not against me is for me."

Leighton illustrates the phenomenon of denominational splits with the metaphor of a rope let down from heaven. "That rope was Christ. The rope has, so to speak, become unraveled at the end. Each of the churches has hold of one strand. Certain churches espouse a certain doctrine of baptism . . . another holds a singular view of spiritual gifts . . . still another believes in a different form of church government. These all say of their agencies, 'Ours is the rope.' But, no—theirs is only one strand of the rope. The rope is Christ. Someday when God pulls that rope up we're going to be surprised by who goes along, even though they weren't holding on to our particular strand.

"In our crusades, we seek to give clear emphasis to the essential truths of the gospel, and not get into issues that divide our brothers and sisters in Christ. At the same time we want to give a witness to our basic unity in Christ. John's Gospel, in chapters thirteen and seventeen, teaches that people will know we are disciples by our love for one another. They will judge Jesus Christ by our unity because Jesus said, 'I pray that you might be one, that the world may believe that the Father has really sent me into the world.' "

Leighton sees this cleavage changing. "An increasing cross section of churches is open to our crusades. They recognize the need for this confrontation with Christ. Young people today are turning in droves to eastern religions and cults . . . looking for community and belonging . . . wanting a challenge . . . hungry for God."

Why does he ask people to "come forward" to express a commitment to Christ?

"You don't have to come forward to be converted but you *do* need to confess Christ publicly. Baptism is, of course, the biblically ordained sign of identification with Christ. Coming forward in a crusade is an open demonstration of an inner commitment—like saluting the flag. The crusade responder is saying, 'I am coming forward with my feet as I come to Christ with my heart.' "

What happens to converts?

"They are encouraged to progress spiritually in several ways. First, a counselor shares with them some material prepared by the Billy Graham Evangelistic Association. We give them a Bible study plan. Forms which they fill out are sent to the pastor of their church, if they have a preference. If they have none, we send their name to a cooperating church near their home. If a person is a member of a noncooperating church we arrange a special follow-up from among the crusade staff.

"We also have what we call nurture groups—small Bible studies in which leaders encourage people to pray, to study the Scriptures systematically, and to share their faith with others."

The German theologian Helmut Thielicke said as he watched an inquirer at the 1963 Billy Graham Crusade in Los Angeles, "He will never forget this experience. This moment will be in every loaf of bread he bakes from now to the end of his life."

Evangelism—always fresh and new yet always the same. Leighton, ordained in Monroe, North Carolina, in May 1955 by the Presbyterian Church U.S. (Southern), is one of the few clergy commissioned by the denomination to do the work of an evangelist, "in season, out of season, reproving, rebuking, exhorting with all longsuffering."

Longsuffering was needed in the extended Vancouver

Reachout. It looked as though the team would end the second phase of the meetings in that spring of April, 1976, as much as $100,000 in debt. The experimental program had been a thirty-month in-depth involvement of church growth, mass media and crusade outreach in a major metropolitan area. A number of new programs made it more expensive than usual.

Leighton approached Allan C. Emery, Jr., president of the Billy Graham Evangelistic Association. Should they quit early? Should they be content with the first phase of the Reachout and pull back?

"Leighton, is there any question of pride or hurt ego here?" Emery asked. "Why are we in this work? Are we in it for the money? Why did you go to Vancouver in the first place? It's to win people for Jesus Christ. What matters is not the money but the will of God. You do what God wants and he will supply the money."

The work went forward; the fruit was reaped; all bills were paid.

Leighton drew up a Vancouver summary:

"The Reachout was experimental here. I felt that we had failed at several points. We tried to do too many new things too quickly without enough preparation and prayer, and we did make some mistakes.

"The chief mistake, I believe, was what theologians call 'triumphalism'—believing that if we could just come up with the right method and plan thoroughly enough all of Vancouver would be evangelized. Triumphalism leaves out both the fact of our human weaknesses and the exclusive power of God through which—and only through which—we triumph.

"Yet, looking back I can see how God brought to pass some very good things. He taught me lessons about trusting him . . . about planning. . . . Vancouver yielded the 'congregational goals survey' which is used today to help congregations to establish their own specific goals for evangelism. This has been picked up by denominational agencies and refined for their use. Vancouver also developed a study called, 'In the Spirit of Love,' which helps congregations in small groups to study and pray together about what it means to be the people of God. This study has probably had more impact *outside* of Vancouver than it did there where it was first used. In fact, we are about to establish a new phase of our team's work, to make these tools available to local churches even when a crusade is not being held in their area.

"If you don't make mistakes you don't make anything. Out of what seemed to be a disappointment God brought fruit that remains."

*F*AILURE CAN FORECAST SUCCESS

Thank God for the ability to fail!

I have discovered that one of the most freeing parts of being God's person is being free to risk and admit failure! Those of us with the drive to perfectionism need to realize what a ridiculous posture it is. God knows we are not perfect. Our families and friends know it. Inside we realize it too, but we just don't want to admit it to ourselves.

In my own case, perfectionism led me to have a preference for controlled situations, particularly in my earlier years. I learned that I could excel in academics and get top grades — particularly in those subjects that demanded sheer hard work. I was not as much at home in the more creative areas. I learned to excel in public speaking very early, possibly because I felt at ease there while I was not comfortable in the give and take of social relationships with my peers.

Growing up tall, gawky, awkward, and skinny did not help. Neither did an overprotective mother and a timid, usually hesitant father. I did not get a lot of encouragement, but I loved sports. I played hockey in college and basketball in seminary, but I never felt fully confident. Later I took up tennis seriously and became a pretty good player. I found the desire to win burned inside of me. When I won I felt great. When I lost I could get very moody. Friends may have thought that I had a hot temper but actually I was angry at myself.

The desire to excel is, I believe, a God-given drive. It grows from a sense of healthy self-worth. Perfectionism, however, is of a different order. Perfectionism is an unrealistic attempt to achieve false standards that we set for ourselves or we think others set for us, and it grows from a false self-evaluation, usually a sense of inferiority. It usually results in our seeming to *be aloof, cold, better than other people. Or in fact, we may seem very much inferior, and very shy. Basically I guess it comes from taking ourselves too seriously. We become afraid to risk, afraid to fail, afraid to be open with other people. We may achieve, but we don't take joy in it. Discipline chokes our spontaneity. We lose the ability to laugh at ourselves. I have often looked with envy at my youngest son, Kevin—a blithesome spirit who has learned (at least most of the time) to laugh when he misses.*

One of the great things about being a Christian is that God knows us better than we know ourselves. For Christ's sake he accepts us just as we are, and then goes to work to make us what he wants us to be. In Christ, he accepts us as "perfect." That frees us up to admit our weaknesses and limitations and by God's help to change them.

During the spring of 1975 God taught me some great lessons in this regard. I was preaching in a crusade in Tulsa, Oklahoma, and I was gripped by a numbing fear. Every time I stood to speak I had to force myself. It was as if after all these years my confidence was totally shaken. I knew the gospel I was preaching was true. I even knew that people would be helped by it, but I had the strangest feeling—my kids would call it "weird"—that nothing I had to say would be of any conceivable interest or help to anybody. In my heart I was cast down and depressed.

One day I had to go out and speak to an open-air meeting at the university at noon, and all that morning I wrestled with the assignment. I just couldn't seem to get a message. I tried to prepare but nothing would come. I was afraid that the students might laugh. Finally, I got down on my knees in desperation and said, "God, I cannot go out there." And then into my mind came some words that God spoke to Abraham, "Fear not, I am your shield and your exceeding great reward." It was as if God said to me, "Son, go on out there. Don't worry about what they may say or how they may look. I am your shield and I am going to protect you. Don't worry about whether or not you succeed. You matter to me not because you are a preacher or a communicator or because you can put across an effective message, but just because I love you. I made you. I redeemed you. You belong to me. Nobody can take that away."

Insight began to come slowly. I realized that since I had been sixteen years old much of my identity had been tied up with being a communicator, and a good public speaker. If that were taken away then something which was deeply rooted was being taken away and I needed to know that I mattered to God, not because I was gifted, or successful, but simply because he loved me with a love that nothing could change.

That was not the end of the struggle. It took some weeks before I began to come out of it. Even now if I speak and feel I haven't communicated or that the message hasn't taken hold, I can be so hurt that I can go back to my room and literally shake, particularly if I happen to be physically or emotionally tired. But I am beginning to learn in my soul and in my bones what grace really means: that God accepts me as I am, and not as I think I have to be.

Someone has said that the whole world is divided into two classes: those who are working toward acceptance, and those who are working from acceptance. The greatest stress in the world is working toward acceptance, always living with the fear of failure. And paradoxically, it is only as I face my fear of failure, and drop the mask of perfectionism, in the light of God's unconditional acceptance, his unmerited, unqualified, unending love that I become free—free to commence becoming all that God made me to be.

11

JUST AS THEY ARE

The talk-show host seated himself at the microphone of a Vancouver, British Columbia, radio station and took the first call: "Good evening, you're on the air. Go ahead."

"I'm calling about Leighton Ford and Billy Graham down at Empire Stadium. Somebody ought to tell those hot gospeling Yankees to go back home."

The emcee smiled. "You're Monty the Richmond Atheist; I recognize your voice."

"Yeah, and I'd like to ask Billy Graham why he came to Vancouver. Does he think Canadians are worse sinners than people in the United States?"

"Well, first of all, Leighton Ford is a Canadian himself. As for Billy Graham, he's preaching for the final three meetings only. Have you heard him?"

"No, not yet."

"Then before you go on about something you haven't investigated, why don't you get down to the stadium tomorrow evening and find out what Billy is saying?"

"Okay," Monty promised, "I'll do it."

He was good to his word. When the offering plate came by he put in a check for two cents—his "two cents worth."

I must believe in God, he thought as he listened to the sermon. *I've shaken my fist at him so many times that I must believe that he exists.*

He heard the preacher say that if anyone has faith as the grain of a mustard seed he can be converted. That was Monty's last night as an unbeliever. He walked down to the field with the stream of inquirers and stood before the platform. He felt ten feet tall. Later, with the urging of his wife, he phoned the talk show and told the emcee and all who were listening about the remarkable change which had come into his life. He had invested two cents; God had given him eternal life.

David Chamberlain was impressed by the preaching of Leighton Ford in Manchester, England in the early sixties. The Britisher named his new son after Leighton and became an evangelist for the Young Life campaigns of the country. But the cares of this world sprang up in his heart and choked his spiritual growth.

When Leighton returned to England to participate in Billy's Earl's Court Crusade in the late sixties he stepped off the platform one evening and found himself face to face with a greasy, hollow-eyed tramp. The man had matted, gray hair, the stubble of a beard, and filthy clothing.

"Do you remember me?"

Leighton couldn't until the man gave his name. David's happy home was gone. All alone, he had been on his way to the greyhound races that night and had seen the advertisement to the Graham meetings on the subway tube. In a little room behind the auditorium David stammered out his story.

What could Leighton say that this prodigal preacher didn't already know? He read the fifty-first Psalm and knelt with him to pray.

David wept for fifteen minutes. Leighton gave him his handkerchief and it was soon sopping wet. That night David Chamberlain returned to his wife and family. He was later restored to his church fellowship and eventually went back into the ministry—rejoicing all the way. Several years later he was killed in an automobile wreck while visiting in California.

A girl in Manchester told Leighton, "My husband and I lived in the same house for two years without speaking. Since our conversion at your meeting it's as if God has remarried us all over again and put love back into our hearts."

Bud and Sandy Snyder in Rochester, New York, were called to a ministry among prisoners during the Leighton Ford Reachout there. They had been half-hearted Christians who came to know the vitality of the gospel as they began going into Auburn Prison and starting "Living Bible" studies among the inmates.

A farmer in Canberra had been told by the director of a Methodist training school in Sydney, "Harry, you might as well go back to the farm. It's obvious you'll never be a preacher."

Downhearted, discouraged, and penniless the man walked the entire distance from downtown far out to the Sydney Stadium to hear Leighton preach a message on Moses.

Harry was reminded that God gave Moses the eloquence he needed. "I knew God had called me to preach and I wasn't going to give up."

Today the ex-farmer who "obviously" could not read or write or learn well enough to be a preacher is a respected, ordained evangelical clergyman in Australia.

When Leighton addressed the students of Adelaide University in Monash, Australia, during the height of campus rebellion in 1968 he was peppered by paper airplanes the entire time.

Ten years later he returned to Australia. The chaplain told him that two of the students who heard him in 1968 made their commitments to Christ that day and actually handed in their names and addresses written on paper airplanes they had hoped would embarrass the speaker. The Lord had found his mark instead and reached their hearts on that confusing yet triumphant day.

Jim Seymour and Ray Monroe slipped into the gospel tent at Bridgeport, Connecticut, for laughs. What Leighton said from the pulpit "took the smirk off our faces."

"We talked ourselves out of stepping forward that night, but I went back the next day with a lot of questions and a Presbyterian minister answered them all *from the Bible!*" Jim remembers.

"The next night Ray and I stepped forward without hesitation. I've become a missionary to the Yupik Eskimos and Ray is a licensed minister with the Assemblies of God."

In Vancouver, British Columbia, Leighton was invited to speak at a meeting of the Woodcutters' Union and to answer questions. The heart of one man was strangely moved, but he didn't respond until a year later.

"It absolutely blew my mind," he said, "to think that a preacher would come and talk to a Woodcutters' Union meeting."

Today as the manager of a Christian bookstore that man believes it was "just God's plan that I was there." He had argued with the preacher in his mind, objecting to every statement he made. But he could not forget the message and it bore fruit eventually. It was the first and only message like it he had ever heard.

Outdoors on the lawn of a teachers' college in Melbourne the school's leading skeptic stood up and walked toward him when Leighton had finished speaking. The young man was well known as the author of an article in the campus publication which he titled, "Christianity, No!"

"I've been an unbeliever," the skeptic declared, "but today I have accepted Jesus Christ as my Savior. Yes, I've been converted."

As Leighton was leaving a nightly crusade meeting in

Sydney, Australia, he heard someone say, "That's Leighton Ford."

"Yes," he said, and turned around to greet a woman.

"My husband came to Christ through your ministry here in 1961 and he's right over there."

Leighton sought him out in the crowd and found a Les Carter so surprised that he couldn't speak at first.

"What a change it made!" he said finally of his conversion. "Before that I didn't have a penny to my name; I lived to drink and gamble. Now I have a business of my own and I'm a lay preacher. Drinking and gambling are no longer necessary. Christ took care of all that."

Following the 1979 Lancaster County Crusade in Pennsylvania a Mennonite couple told Leighton that they heard another message during the eight-day meeting by the appearance of Mr. and Mrs. Ford.

"We're identified with a simple life style," commented Eugene Witmer of Smoketown, "and this Presbyterian comes in wearing the same suit three nights in a row and the same jacket with sport pants the other nights."

To top it off, Mr. Witmer said, "his wife wore the same dress to three public occasions. That really was quite unsettling for the fashion-conscious Christians who saw a lady of her position so unconcerned about those peripheral matters. It was a subtle humility that Leighton and Jean had no idea they were communicating."

What could Leighton say to forty scholars gathered for the historic evangelical-Jewish dialogue sponsored in New York by the American Institute of Holy Land Studies and the American Jewish Committee? He didn't want to set forth platitudes on brotherhood or to arrogantly turn the meeting into a propaganda session.

Leighton remembered meeting Rabbi Richard Rocklin in Charlotte and decided to invite him to lunch in a

Chinese restaurant and ask what Jews would be interested in hearing from an evangelical.

"Be yourself," the rabbi counseled. "Just get that dialogue off to the right start by speaking at the gut level."

Leighton's message in New York was delivered as a "Letter to Richard," in which the evangelical preacher chronicled his early life and conversion, presenting "solid, historical, and intellectual grounds for faith in Jesus," but also building bridges of friendship to the Jewish leaders present.

"We don't hide the fact that we want you to believe Jesus is the Messiah," Leighton wrote. "We really do. We can't withhold our convictions that he is the fulfillment of the great plan of the God of Abraham, the appearance in history of the Lord himself. . . .

"The first thing I've learned more deeply is how close we really are, to be so far apart." Leighton acknowledged that "from Jewish eyes, maybe the Christian emphasis on faith makes it into a kind of buck-passing irresponsibility. From Christian eyes, the Jewish emphasis on 'Torah' may look like legalism. But is the gap distorted by the spectacles we wear?"

He quoted one of the Jewish scholars at the dialogue who had said earlier, "The Jew is fully aware that no man can pass muster before God if he rests his case on law . . . rather than on the unmerited mercy of God."

"King David's experience of pardoning grace as he records it in Psalm 32 is cast in words that find an echo in my own spirit. May I ask if you do not also respond to Jesus' words that he had come not to destroy but to fulfill the Law? When he said that he came that we might have life abundantly, was he not affirming Torah—life to the full?

"I've learned in a deeper way that what is very precious to us may be offensive to you. I'm wondering how many of my Christian brothers and sisters realize that while Good Friday is a holy day to us, it is a day on which for many years and in many places a Jew was slapped on both cheeks? How many of us know that there were times when Jews were forced by law to go to churches and listen to sermons aimed at converting them?

". . . Many people who call themselves Christians are reflecting cultural patterns, not biblical principles. Don't imagine that everyone calling himself a Christian is one. There are multitudes of people who are only 'cultural Christians,' not biblical ones.

". . . We are open to a diversity of responses to the lordship of Jesus Christ, recognizing there are Jews who accept him yet who wish to remain within Jewish culture and tradition.

"And who knows what God might do to bridge the gulf between us, which no man can bridge? I do not suggest that we abridge our deep convictions. I do dare to believe that the day will come when by God's grace the natural and wild branches will be joined in the olive tree. Then, and then alone, will the universal mission of the people of God be carried out."

Leighton drew hearty laughs at Columbia Seminary when he kicked off a 1968 winter lecture series: "I noticed this evening that it was foggy when I arrived at the airport and the closer I got to the seminary the foggier it got."

But the students roared when President J. McDowell Richards shot back, "Well, Leighton, it wasn't foggy until you got here!"

In 1970, Leighton casually met Doug Bell, a Charlotte anchor man for Channel 9, then the local NBC affiliate WSOC-TV.

"Leighton, when I get through with the news it's usually so bad I want to say, 'Let us pray!' " Bell commented.

"But I can't do that. *You* could, however. Why don't you prepare something short—something inspirational—that we could put as a trailer?"

Leighton liked the idea and tried to get Billy to do it, but his brother-in-law threw it back on his shoulders. In about a year, Leighton was ready with several writers to assist and a collection of one-minute TV spots. The feature, first called "Insight" and later changed to "The Leighton Ford TV Feature," is distributed to forty-five television stations across the United States. Jo Boynton handles the distribution of the tapes from an office in her Charlotte home.

(Except for the help he gets on this television program and for a similar program he does on Australian radio, Leighton conducts all of his own research for his writing and for the preparation of sermons, articles, and books.)

Response to the TV feature was immediate. A suicidal elderly woman in Gastonia, North Carolina, found hope and turned away from a plan to end her life.

A television repairman told his customer, "I'm an atheist but Leighton Ford makes more sense than anyone I've ever heard on television."

An alcoholic stopped Leighton downtown. "Hey, you don't know me, but I gotta tell you something. When you did that little thing on alcoholism I needed it bad. I turned my life over to God, and you know what? I got a job and I've been able to quit drinking."

A lady in Charlotte had been watching Leighton on television and when she met him on the street one day she said, "I really like your program but there's just one thing."

"What's that?" Leighton asked.

"You're so much better looking on television than you are in person."

"Thank you," Leighton said.

She did a double take. "Oh, no! I didn't mean that, I meant just the opposite!"

That wasn't much better but Leighton thanked her again.

Trying to pay him a compliment, she put another foot in her mouth: "How long is it, it's five minutes, isn't it?"

"No, it just lasts one minute."

"Oh," she replied, "it seems much longer."

A Christian writer for Leighton's TV news feature sent his copy one day with a note that he would not be writing any more. "I'm just not sure I still believe it," he said.

Leighton sat down at his typewriter and sent a personal note. This is how his message was received:

"I don't know what response I expected from Leighton but, well, what I received was terrific. A letter he had typed himself—full of typos—with nothing but encouragement and love. The words were not nearly as important as the spirit. He showed that he understood, firsthand, the clouds that were around me, and offered love and care and prayer. . . . It was the *personal* love and warmth that made such an impact. Later, when the clouds passed, and I wrote to tell him, his reply was short and sweet: 'Hallelujah! When do you start writing again?' "

On January 12, 1969, his partnership with Billy Graham was expanded as he began taking every other week's broadcast of "The Hour of Decision." Billy had carried it for twenty years and needed time for other responsibilities.

Leighton's first broadcast was titled, "This Is Progress?" In it he described a mythical visitor from a century ago to the United States today. The visitor went away concluding that this nation had houses without homes, speed without direction, medicine without health, knowledge without wisdom, communication without understanding, and entertainment without happiness.

"This," Leighton asked, "is progress?"

Leighton Ford in Australia talking with a young aborigine woman and her child.

12

A SOCIAL CONSCIENCE

The Leighton Ford Crusades' Reachout is a hand reached up and a hand reached out. "It's a hand reached up to receive from God his grace, forgiveness, and salvation; it's also a hand reached out to share that love of Jesus Christ in practical ways with others."

The evangelist believes there is no such thing as a "social gospel." There is only one gospel which is social as well as personal. Jesus dealt with the whole person. He died on the cross to forgive sins and to give eternal life. He fed hungry people and healed the sick.

The Leighton Ford Crusaders call this emphasis "Christian Action"—an affirmation of the new birth through good works.

In Rochester, New York, following the Attica Prison Riots of 1972, a permanent program called "Bridge" was established with funds collected by Reachout. Christians went into Attica and Auburn Prisons to befriend inmates and to help them to get a job and a place to stay when released. The Commissioner of Corrections for New York told crusade chairman Bill Showalter that the state-wide rate of recidivism in New York of 60 percent fell in the Rochester area to 35 percent largely because of the concern of Christian people growing out of the crusade.

In Rockford, Illinois, one of the "Christian Action" projects was the sponsorship of a chaplain in the Rockford jail. Funds came from the Reachout there initially.

In Des Moines, Iowa, Christians involved in the Leighton Ford crusade built information booths in the auditorium where the various social agencies working with human need could explain their programs and recruit helpers.

In Lancaster, Pennsylvania, a post-crusade dinner of rice and tea for $50 a plate raised $46,000 for ministry among Indochina's rootless "boat people" suffering and dying adrift in the South China Sea. The money was dispatched through the Billy Graham World Emergency Fund to evangelical agencies working in the area.

After the Berlin World Congress on Evangelism other congresses sprang up in various parts of the world. The U.S. Congress on Evangelism was held in September 1969 at Minneapolis. American society was splintering into subcultures, precipitated largely by civil injustices and by resistance against the Indochina War.

In the climate of change characterized by street riots, hippies, yippies, and flower power Leighton was asked to keynote the congress with a message on "The Church and Evangelism in a Day of Revolution." His message was prophetic and response was instant and intense. Leighton felt that he "spoke beyond myself" about things he felt needed to be said.

"What has evanglism to do with revolution?" he asked. "Just this—that Christ's work never goes on in a vacuum, and today the Christian church is being called to evangelize people caught up in cataclysmic change.

"The strange plight of modern man is that while his knowledge is exploding, the whole idea of 'true truth'—truth which is the opposite of falsehood—is disappearing. In art, philosophy, theology, and the total pattern of his thinking, twentieth century man seeks to escape from reason. Everything is relative. This has led inevitably to a moral revolution, the shift from an absolute ethic to a situation ethic, from a morality based on God's eternal law to one based on man's personal 'likes.' "

The evangelist noted the changes compounded by the communications revolution . . . pointed out that children of the electronic age are the first generation to know more than their parents . . . warned that Christians "dare not be blind to the lesson all modern revolutions have taught: when men of privilege abuse their power, and refuse justice, sooner or later upheaval will come."

He called it "shameful" that the Christian church has been so slow to face the demands of the gospel in the racial revolution of our time. "With some notable exceptions," he said, "we have moved only when we have been run over from behind. We have enjoyed, many of us, our privileged position at the 'white hand of God.' "

He called early Christians "revolutionaries, Christian style," and termed their Master *"a revolutionary God,* releasing *revolutionary power* through a *revolutionary community* in a *revolutionary action.* . . .

"The Church stands with all mankind at a common crossroad, sharing a common concern: which way do we go to make a new world? There are some who say, '*Learn*—education is the way.' Some say, '*Earn*—economic development will solve our problems.' Some voices are crying, '*Burn*—society is so corrupt we must destroy it.' But Jesus Christ says, '*Turn.*' Be converted. Put your trust in God. Seek first his will. Then you can be part of the new world God is making."

Leighton summarized his thoughts: "God's revolution is going to go on, with or without you and me. But I don't want to get left behind. So this is my prayer: *Lord, start a revolution, and start it in me!*"

Oswald J. Hoffmann, the moderator, took the podium after Leighton's message and asked, "Dr. Graham, do you have anything to say?"

"All I can say is 'Amen!' " Billy responded.

Before the U.S. Congress on Evangelism had ended Leighton had an opportunity to practice what he was preaching. Just before Keith Miller was to speak one evening in the cavernous municipal auditorium a couple of hippies walked down the center aisle and sat on the floor in front of the platform. The ushers were instructed to take them out (fire laws, security, etc.). The hippies wouldn't go, so they were picked up and carried out amid boos and protests from the crowd.

Keith began his address, said a few witty things, then stopped: "I'm really hacked. Here we are talking about evangelism and two people who look most like Jesus here tonight have been taken out."

The remarks threatened to unravel the unity of the congress. Leighton, seated in the gallery, got up with a couple of friends and went out looking for the hippies. He found them in a room on the side where some people were trying to calm them down. He talked with them for a long time until finally they agreed to go back into the meeting. They went back, walked to the front and sat on the floor together. There was a warm response and a burst of applause.

Time and *Newsweek* editorialized about the dramatic issues set forth in Minneapolis by the evangelicals. Some tried to put distance between Billy and Leighton, saying the younger evangelist was socially concerned and the older evangelist was not.

"Perhaps Billy and I do perceive social issues from slightly different perspectives for various reasons—age, background, nationality, theology. I come from the Reformed tradition which has always put a strong emphasis on relating our faith to the lordship of Christ over our total lives, including culture, society, and so forth. But our viewpoints are not that different. It's a difference of perspective only, not one of conviction. Billy's early unsegregated crusades in the South gave tremendous impetus to the entire civil rights movement."

Leighton reaped other reactions from that message. He learned from Allan Emery that some people had concluded that Leighton Ford did not believe in the divine inspiration of the Scriptures.

Leighton was stunned. "Allan, why would anyone think that? I've never in my life said anything close to that. I believe totally in the authority of the Scriptures."

"Well, it's because of your social emphasis. People don't think you can have social concern and still be true to the Scriptures."

"But Allan, my concern comes out of the Bible—out of the prophets . . . out of what Jesus taught and what the apostles believed. It's because I believe in the authority of Scripture that I think we have to believe all that the Bible teaches."

"I know that, but I'm telling you what's been said and what some people think. They have concluded that you must be going liberal. They can't yet associate social concern with evangelistic concern and see how it comes out of the same Scriptures."

Evangelicals—at least in lip service—have come a long way since those early days of change. Leighton alluded to this in his book *One Way to Change the World.*

One year after the Minneapolis Congress, Leighton was involved in the opposite side of the twin emphases of social concern and spiritual rebirth. Paul Little, as he studied the format of Urbana 70, the triennial missionary conference sponsored by Inter-Varsity Christian Fellowship at Urbana, Illinois, decided that the conference might come down too heavily on social issues and needed the balance of solid theological preaching on "The Lostness of Man." The person to preach it, he reasoned, was the evangelical who had a social conscience and who expressed it publicly—Leighton Ford.

Inter-Varsity's David Howard came to similar conclusions while writing *Student Power and Evangelism.* In the early twenties there had been a split between the Inter-Varsity Christian Fellowship and the Student Volunteer Movement over the issue of the authority of Scripture and on evangelism and social action. Howard and Little were determined that the same thing would not happen in Inter-Varsity groups. They accurately predicted that tension would develop among evangelical students living in the era of existential freedom. Leighton's sermon at Urbana was to remind the students of the eternal peril facing lost souls and an individual's need for salvation.

The night before Leighton spoke black evangelist Tom Skinner had brought the thirteen thousand students to their feet in the huge oval auditorium at the University of Illinois, stomping and cheering. Some wanted to turn Urbana 70 into a Christian activist crusade. Blacks were leading the thrust and certain of them cornered Paul Little angrily because he wouldn't uncork this tremendous surge and let it flow in all of its force.

Leighton's message on eternal judgment for unbelievers clarified the issues of Christian evangelism in light of the lostness of individuals.

"As believers," Leighton said, "our approach must be clear-eyed and perceptive. Our faith must be rooted in the one eternal gospel, relevant to the world in which we live this faith. To neglect either is a denial of our Bible, our history, our belief—indeed, of our Lord."

13

LEIGHTON AND BILLY

During the 1975 Christmas season Leighton telephoned the unlisted number which is periodically changed and drove again the winding lane up Black Mountain overlooking Montreat. He had turned forty-four. Offers of important leadership positions in the Christian world were being presented to him.

"I know why you've come," Billy said. "You're at that time of life when you are restless about the future, about the opportunities facing you which require decisions, about the imposed tensions of 'What will Billy think?' which people place on everything you say and do."

Leighton relaxed. It was a scene replayed. Twenty-six years earlier on a frigid night in Chatham Billy had become an esteemed—virtually idolized—mentor to a seventeen-year-old protégé. Providence had drawn the two into a common association, into the same family, into a constant comparison of beliefs, emphases, and even appearances. An acquaintance who is a psychologist suggests that Billy had become a stand-in father for Leighton's adoptive parent, who had been largely ineffective.

Earlier in their association Leighton had practiced aloofness from Billy, fearing that he would be a bother. He rarely phoned, hardly ever wrote, did not attend a Billy Graham Crusade unless assigned to a specific task, and deferred to Billy in board meetings.

That began to change. Leighton found himself sharing with Billy what he was doing and Billy in turn did the same. Leighton's loyalty has always been complete. In the face of endless invitations to serve in other capacities

Leighton has remained: "An associate evangelist of the Billy Graham Evangelistic Association."

Leighton's voluntary distance from Billy, knowing his heavy schedule and seeking to avoid the artificiality that characterized people who maneuver to impress or to gain favor with celebrities, might have been commendable except that it was often misunderstood.

"Your dislike of politicking is commendable, Leighton," Allan Emery told him, "but in the process you have earned the reputation of being aloof, reserved, withdrawn. Integrity is important but it's not enough just to have integrity. It can become too important. The cultivation of other people can become something that is viewed as being beneath you, so you end up being misread. That has been one of your problems even on our board."

("Faithful are the wounds of a friend.")

Another associate coveted for Leighton more visibility. "I feel for him," he said. "It isn't always easy for Leighton to determine what God wants him to do. Billy has always been forthright on proclamation. He gets involved in a world congress on evangelism at a level which doesn't cost him anything in terms of image. But Leighton tends to become submerged."

Sandy's health crisis probably did more than any other single event to relax Leighton's image of a controlled, reserved cleric. He emerged from the vigil as a person who could weep, as a perfectionist who didn't have everything in place after all, as a father whose heart could be broken by circumstances beyond his control.

Has Leighton's ministry been hindered or enhanced by being in the shadow of Billy Graham? Leighton is not a go-it-alone type. He prefers to work with a team. The opportunity of enjoying all that BGEA has to offer, of employing the efficiencies that Executive Vice President George Wilson has developed—it's all been a golden experience.

"I worked very much in the background during those early crusades," says Leighton, "but I had fantastic opportunities that never would have come to me if it hadn't been for the association with Billy. I think of the crusades in Canada after the 1955 Toronto meeting; the opportunity at the age of twenty-five to direct all the church relations for the New York Crusade; the huge crowds to which I preached in Jamaica in 1958; Australia in 1959; taking Billy's place in Manchester in 1961—none of this would have come if it hadn't been for the opportunity to work with Billy. Thankfully, I had a background in Christian work that kept me from being a novice."

Jean believes that her husband's association with her brother has been "a tremendous asset, yes, and I think Billy has had to hold back a little bit in promoting Leighton simply because Leighton is his brother-in-law. Leighton has tried to lead, even at the risk of being misunderstood.

"Maybe his reluctance to take that front seat . . . maybe his lack of initiative in phoning Billy when everybody else was flooding him . . . maybe his refusing to go to a crusade unless he could contribute—these could have been interpreted as an attempt to pull away from Billy, but it wasn't," Jean adds.

The wife and sister noted other comparisons:

"Leighton almost never alludes to his health (which is excellent) while Billy almost always does among friends. Is Billy's preoccupation with his health a compensation because he is called upon by a supportive public to be almost superhuman?

"When Billy calls here to chat you know he's through when he says, 'Well. . . .' You might just as well hang up. He's finished. In a meeting you know Billy Frank is through listening when he begins to make little clicking sounds with his tongue. Leighton tends to hear a person out, no matter how long it takes.

"The other side of the coin in this matter of Leighton's

association with BGEA is that he has contributed much to the organization."

Billy is the first to say this about the whole image of the association worldwide. At a team meeting he introduced Leighton as "one who has become much more than an associate. He's become a world evangelist who represents the Billy Graham team. He is a man like Nathaniel, without guile."

Neither man is a grabber and a hugger. Billy will occasionally kick his pal Grady Wilson on the leg and ask what the matter is with pretended disgust. Billy used to shake his sister's hand. Now he gives her a bear hug.

"I write him little notes as only a sister could," she says, "because he rarely gets that kind of mail. That means much to him. So many people want something all the time. . . .

"People ask me ridiculous questions like: 'Who is the best preacher, Billy or Leighton?' "

(Leighton asked her, "Well, who *is* the best preacher?" and she replied, "Depends what day it is and what the subject is!")

Occasionally a stranger will say to Jean, "We really like your husband better than Billy Graham."

"How am I supposed to answer? I reply, 'I'm Billy's sister by birth and Leighton's wife by choice.' "

At family gatherings in Charlotte "Billy does the talking," his sister Catherine reports. Melvin can be as loquacious when he gets rolling. For Leighton, who had no kin for so many years, each reunion is special.

Ruth Graham sent a letter: "Leighton is a barrel of fun in family gatherings, always courteous and considerate, interested in everyone, an interesting conversationalist with a keen sense of humor. Also, his example as a husband and father is an inspiration to the whole family."

As farmer Melvin spread manure fertilizer on the flower bed of a customer, the woman watched him for a while then began to laugh. "Aren't you Billy Graham's brother?" she asked.

"Yes. Billy's out saving those poor souls and I'm here saving your poor soil."

Twice Leighton has been involved in situations that strained his comradeship with Billy. One involved Billy's retirement; the other was a misunderstanding in preparation for a team meeting.

In an interview with a Dallas, Texas, newspaper a reporter asked, "Is Billy Graham going to continue these large-scale crusades?" In his reply Leighton quoted Billy's statement (made both in public and in private) that he didn't know how long he could continue the stadium crusades because they took so much out of him physically. Leighton added that he thought Billy probably would not continue his big city-wide crusades but would, rather, concentrate on television and smaller efforts indoors, which is exactly what Billy had said.

"I also told the reporter that I felt that in the future, mass evangelism would involve more work with local churches and not only the big crusades. I believe that strongly and Billy believes that. BGEA has always emphasized work with the churches and is increasing this emphasis. But the headlines shouted: 'Billy Graham Getting Ready to Retire.' The story said that Billy would stop his crusades and then Leighton's methods would take over. It appeared that we were not going to have mass evangelism but rather church-related outreaches—complete misinterpretation."

T. W. Wilson called Leighton from Dallas where Billy was going through and had seen the headline. "Leighton," he said, "what in the world. . . ."

"I told him what happened. But afterward in press conferences this issue of retirement would keep coming up. I could tell Billy was nettled."

The second problem arose during a 1973 meeting of

the associate evangelists. In preparation for that meeting a survey was prepared to determine what kind of preparation and on-the-job training associate evangelists needed for their work. This report would go into the material being prepared by Leighton and a team of specialists for the new Billy Graham Center then taking shape.

Two members of the staff drew up the questionnaire and had it duplicated and distributed. Billy asked some outsiders to attend the meeting and that questionnaire was handed to them also without prior clearance. One of the questions related to whether people felt that their superiors in the association understood them, and whether there were changes they would like to have in the team meetings to make them more effective.

Billy saw a copy of the questionnaire and felt that it might be misinterpreted. He ordered that all the questionnaires be gathered up and not used. It was a misunderstanding, but he made it clear that he accepts his responsibility for determining what goes on at his team meetings.

Any disagreement has to be kept in perspective. Pastor Calvin Thielman has been close to Billy for sixteen years and has never heard anything but Billy's highest praise for Leighton's ability and dedication.

At a 1978 meeting of the team, Billy introduced Leighton as the opening speaker:

Always at these meetings we have held for many years . . . I have given the opening address. This year I felt led to ask Leighton Ford. I do not know anyone who has his fingers on the pulse of the world church or has a greater vision of what we ought to be and ought to do and ought to emphasize more than Leighton.

Leighton is a remarkable person in so many ways. He is a man of God in whom there is no guile. I was asked by representatives that are raising money what would happen if Billy Graham were to die, or if I would be killed if a plane went down. What would happen to the Billy Graham Association? Our plan is, under God, that Leighton Ford would take responsibilities of leading. Leighton is a great evangelist, a great preacher, a great strategist in his own right. I have seen results almost from the time he graduated from seminary. His fellowship and his friendship, his love, his counsel and his advice have meant more to me personally than I can possibly express to you.

He has been with us twenty-two years and during that time he has grown far beyond being a member of BGEA or an Associate Evangelist as he came with us to be. He has come to be a churchman and a church leader with a world stature. We are very proud of him, and we thank God for him. Leighton, you come.

Leighton Ford and Billy Graham—"evangelist, brother-in-law, brother."

"WHAT IS BILLY LIKE?"

If you asked me to name the people who have had the greatest influence on my life I would say without hesitation my mother, my wife Jeanie, and my brother-in-law, Billy Graham.

He was instrumental in leading me into the two most important aspects of my life—next to my faith in Jesus Christ: my marriage to Jeanie and my ministry.

People sometimes have asked me whether I mind being in "Billy's shadow," or playing "second fiddle" to Billy. If I am in his shadow it is a mighty grand shadow to walk in. Billy does not try to cramp anyone's style by making them play second fiddle. He has always encouraged me and the other associate evangelists on the Billy Graham Team in our own ministry, and has done everything he could to strengthen and help us. He is our unquestioned leader—but he has always tried so much to be a sensitive leader, that it is a stimulating experience to serve with him.

"What is Billy Graham like?" I am often asked.

When I first met him I was impressed by both his public and his private sides. The public Billy is the model God used to shape my ministry. I can still remember the first times I heard him preach—at the Youth for Christ Conventions at Winona Lake, Indiana, and at the Canadian Youth Fellowship Conferences. I would have been only sixteen or seventeen at the time, at that impressionable time when boys need heroes.

Billy was a spiritual hero to me, no doubt about it. There was something about the way he preached that made him unique. It wasn't just his oratorical style (there were others who could match him in drama, pathos, and eloquence). Nor was it the blue gabardine suit and the hand-painted tie. It was the sheer intensity, the white-hot flame, the total sense of being wrapped up in what he was doing so that the messenger and the message seemed like one. This was what caught and captivated his audience, including this teenage boy. Billy has always tended to be crisis-oriented and there was an urgency in his message that I believe God used to precipitate the spiritual crisis. I once heard him preach to a packed church in Chicago out of an Old Testament text about "the spirit of burning." Billy was like the bush that burned and was not consumed.

He incarnated for me the ministry of "the evangelist." I had heard my mother talk about a meeting she attended as a girl with the famous evangelist, R. A. Torrey, in Buffalo when the crowds sang on the streetcars to and from the meetings. I probably heard a few traveling evangelists, but in Billy and many of those around him in Youth for Christ I saw what an evangelist could be in the hands of God—a man who preached for a verdict. I wanted to be like him. I had used him as a model to stir in my own heart the recognition of my gift as an evangelist. Like many other young preachers in those days I wanted to be like Billy. I probably copied him in my style in those early days. It was like a would-be baseball player who imitated Mickey Mantle—hitching his pants as he did, perching his cap on his head as he did, trying to swing his bat as he did. We all have to model ourselves after someone and I tried to follow Billy as he followed Jesus.

If a ball player really has it he will start patterning himself after someone else and then go on to develop his own groove and style. I believe that is also true in the Christian life. Most of us have a spiritual mentor who guides us in the early days, but then as we grow and mature through life, we begin to find the uniqueness that God has built into each of our personalities. Just as salt brings out the individual flavor of each kind of food, so Jesus Christ does not make us into Christian puppets but rather brings out the individuality for which we were created. The more I become like Jesus Christ, the more I become like my true self. In later years I have developed more and more my own particular style of communication which God has given to me. I probably do less preaching at people and more preaching with them. That is, I tend to combine strong authoritative proclama-

tion with personal sharing. The stamp that God put on my life through Billy will always be there I am sure, and I will always be thankful for it.

The private Billy is one most people don't get to see. But I have been privileged to know him on intimate terms both on our team and in our family. He is as engaging in private as he is in public. His mind is a steel trap, hardly ever forgetting anything. I am constantly amazed at how much he remembers and knows—not only about our work but about what is going on around the world.

Because of the sheer force and magnetism of his personality, and all the fascinating experiences he has, Billy tends to dominate or control most conversations. I have also learned that if you want to speak to him about something you have to choose the time. When he gets through with a conversation it's almost as if something clicks in his mind and he is tuned out—and no wonder, with the myriad of things he has pushing in upon him.

But I have also found him to be a good and compassionate listener. I will never forget how he put his arm around me when I was crying with disappointment on the stage at the Chatham Collegiate Institute, and how he encouraged me to keep that burden for people that God had given. My mother was opposed to my marriage to Jeanie—at least until I got my doctorate. That would have postponed our marriage for several years. I remember going up into Billy's office in their old house at Montreat and talking with him about it. He listened, he understood, he asked some probing questions and he told me that, though the decision was mine, there would have to come a time when I would have to cut those apron strings.

Billy can be tough when he needs to be. I have heard him speak with steel in his voice. But he is perhaps the most generous man that I have ever known whether in terms of forgiving or overlooking someone's faults or helping them in an area of weakness, or being willing to assist in a financial need. Sometimes his generosity has gotten him in trouble! But it is also one of the secrets of his greatness.

In the last several years our relationship has entered a new *phase. I no longer look at us as a boy and his coach, but more on a one-to-one relationship. It has been a privilege to discuss and counsel with him about many of our major undertakings together. We write and talk to each other on the phone much more frequently.*

And I have learned that a man who is great and famous can be very lonely. One afternoon recently in Australia I went up to his room. I was leaving for the United States and I wanted to tell him good-bye. His wife, Ruth, had left several days earlier. I got up several times to take my farewell but he asked me, "Please stay, don't leave." So I stayed on even though the time was coming when he had to leave shortly for the evening meeting, and when I left he asked me to pray and I put my arm around him and he laid his head on my shoulder and put his arm around me as I prayed for him.

To a young life which had not known the guidance of a father or the companionship of brothers, God sent me a prize in the form of Billy Graham—evangelist, brother-in-law, brother.

TO MY UNKNOWN PARENTS

It seems strange to be writing to a mother and father I've never known—not knowing for certain your names, where you live, or even if you are still living. I can only hope that you will somehow see what I write.

Not until several years ago did I start to be interested in discovering my roots. But recently I have started to wonder about you and how I might find out about you. It seemed as if looking for you would be a hopeless cause. We had so little to go on—a hint dropped here and there by my adoptive parents, some bits of seemingly contradictory information they had passed on to one family friend or another. The laws of Ontario, Canada, also seemed to offer little chance of tracing my origins.

But then my good colleague and friend, Stan Izon, stepped into the picture. Stan lives in Toronto and is himself fascinated by genealogies. He has traced his family tree back many generations and when he learned of my growing interest in looking into my past, it sparked his own curiosity. Stan and his wife Shirley have been a great help as they have spent many leisure hours talking to doctors, hospital authorities, and family lawyers. They have cross-checked various archives and records to see if one of the possible clues would check out. Had my father been an attorney or perhaps from a fairly well-known family of manufacturers? Was my mother the daughter of a clergyman? Did the "McCrea" that my mother had informally added to my name during my teenage years have some significance?

At first nothing seemed to turn up. Then Stan came across a very kind and helpful lady in Toronto who works for an organization which seeks to help adopted children locate their parents. She told him of a recent law which permitted an adopted child, once the adopting parents were dead, to apply for a copy of the adoption orders.

Stan drew up the necessary application and we supplied the required documentation to the authorities. Frankly, I didn't expect much since the previous leads had continually come to dead ends.

Then in December 1979 Stan and I were in Chicago to take part in a conference near O'Hare airport. After our meetings were over he came to my room and with no word of warning passed over an envelope. "This will interest you," he said.

I pulled out an official looking piece of paper and for the first time read my natural-born name.

Leighton Frederick Sandys Ford had been born as Peter Morgan _____.

"In the case of Peter Morgan _____, registered under the vital Statistics Act as _____ with no Christian name. . . ."

As my children would say, mine was a "weird" feeling that night. Who was I really? Leighton or Peter? And how did the Leighton as whom I had known myself for four and one-half decades relate to the Peter of my past? Was I registered with my mother's maiden or married name? The paper also noted that the adoption had been approved by the Supreme Court of Ontario which suggested some unusual circumstance.

I shared my discovery with an Irish friend who told me in delight that I had a true Gaelic name, and could be either Scottish or Irish, Protestant or Catholic. His book of Gaelic names indicated that my name could mean "the dark-headed man who makes peace."

Now the question faces me: do I really want to trace this any further? If I could, would I wish to arrange a meeting with you? Would you want this? Or would it dredge up painful memories that are best left alone? And why have I gone this far anyway?

Has psychological need played a part? It may be that coming to the mid-time of my life has awakened an urge to know where I've come from. Yet I cannot say I have sensed an impelling drive *along these lines. After all, I long ago came to know and believe that my ultimate origin and roots are with my heavenly Father.*

I think that above all, I'd like to tell the two of you who conceived me and brought me to birth, if we ever do meet, the wonder of God's leading in my life. I'd like you to know more about what this book tells about . . . how God led me to an adoptive family where I first heard about Jesus and his love and saving grace . . . how I came to know him as my Savior as a small boy and grew to know him as my guiding Lord. I'd like to tell you more about the kind of ministry God has given, and the multiplied thousands of lives I've had the privilege of touching around the world. I'd like for you to know Billy Graham, not as a public figure, but in the warm and human way I've come to know and love him. It would be so good if you could meet Jeanie and know what a fine, deep, wise, and compassionate person she is and the kind of security and fulfillment God has given us in our covenant with each other. And what if you could meet three grandchildren you've never known you had! I'd love so much for you to get to know Debbie, with her beauty and strong, outgoing personality . . . Sandy, so dedicated and firm, so high-principled, so full of plans and dreams . . . and Kevin, with his fantastic mind and memory, and his quick wit that keeps us all laughing and happy. As the old hymn says, I'd like you to "see what God can do"!

I have tried to put myself back into your situation. What must it have been like for you from the time you learned in early 1931 that I was on the way until I was born that October twenty-second?

It's difficult to imagine, Mother, what you must have gone through—your struggles way back in 1931. And you, Father, did you share in that sense of regret and responsibility? Why did you decide to give me up for adoption and how hard was that decision? Did you make it together? (One thing I am deeply grateful for: you didn't take the "easy" way out—abortion. Thank you and thank God!)

As I have thought of my own three children, I have sought to feel what it must be like to bring a baby to birth and then say good-bye to it, probably forever. Has time buried those memories deep? Have you forgotten or do you still wonder what happened to that boy baby?

In any case, I decided to close this book with a letter to you in the sheer hope that sometime, somehow, you will read it and learn the rest of the story. If ever I do learn where you are, I pledge in my own heart not to force a meeting unless you and I are both convinced that this is right.

But I really do want you to know how things turned out. "Let bygones be bygones," they say. But bygones *don't always lead to* foregone *conclusions. Out of painful experiences good can come. I believe that because I believe in the God who has surprised me so often, for he is the true and living God. The Bible tells the story of Joseph being sold into slavery in Egypt by his brothers who then concocted a story about a wild animal slaying him. Years later his brothers were astounded to find that he had become one of the leaders of Egypt, a wise man, who by his foresight and planning saved hundreds of lives from death by starvation. "You meant it for evil," Joseph told them, "but God meant it for good."*

With even greater wonder I think how God took the worst thing that man ever did—putting the Son of God to death on a cross—and redeemed that damnable deed to bring about the best thing that was ever done for man—our eternal salvation!

What a great God of wonders he is—so often surprising us! As I reflect back on my life so far, that truth stands out clearly for me. As your son I wish to thank you for giving me life by telling you of the Christ who offers to you and me eternal life. Someday I hope I might have the privilege of telling you about this in person.

Looking back to my roots has also given me a quiet sense of confidence about the future. Just as my past is partly a mystery, so is my future. Though I don't understand all the Bible tells about the believer's destiny, I do believe that I will go to heaven to be with Christ . . . even to be like him! But there's so much unknown about all that is going to happen between now and then. Someone has said the Christian is rather like a man who comes into a movie at the very end and then sits through the next showing. He knows what the end will be, but not how the plot will get there! So the Bible tells me that Jesus Christ will be the Omega Point of history. When he comes, God's kingdom will fully arrive on earth in all its beauty, power and glory. Until then there will be wars, earthquakes, famines, disasters as well as a growing impact of the gospel. Good and evil will both increase and conflict will intensify, but God will bring down history's final curtain.

Looking back, there is so much I would like to know, but don't. Looking ahead, I feel very much the same. Sometimes I wish I could just turn on a video tape and replay my whole past from the time before I was born. But that might not be helpful. So looking in the other direction, if we really could have video-tape scenes from our future life, would that be so good? Must God not have very good and wise reasons for limiting our horizons?

At this point it is enough to know that God can take me into an unknown future just as he brought me from an unknown past. And I expect him to keep right on surprising me. After all, as one of my friends says, "God really is God. He's not applying for the job!"

Without this confidence that God really is sovereign and knows the beginning from the end, I don't see how any of us can face the future with the growing prospect of political struggles, nuclear war, surging inflation, energy problems, moral conflicts. I look at our three children and would have a sense of dread for their future unless I knew that I could safely entrust them to this God who works in a mysterious way to perform his wonders, knowing he has their times in his hands as he has had mine. I don't know all the future holds as far as my ministry is concerned. Opportunities have come in other directions which have been very challenging—to be editor of a major Christian journal, the president of a seminary, and so forth. Jeanie and I haven't sensed these as God's calling for now. So I continue with the calling of preaching and teaching, of working for world evangelism, and of encouraging young people in these areas, believing that he will open and close doors with perfect timing. As Jeanie and I have experienced together the renewing and deepening of our love, so we are confident that he will continue to enrich and bless our lives and ministries together.

Just this morning before I wrote this I was struck by these words from the fortieth chapter of Isaiah: "Why do you say, O Jacob, and complain, O Israel, 'My way is hidden from the Lord; My cause is disregarded by my God'? Do you not know? Have you not heard? The Lord is the everlasting God, the Creator of the ends of the earth. He will not grow tired or weary, and his understanding no one can fathom. He gives strength to the weary and increases the power of the weak. Even youths grow tired and weary, and young men stumble and fall; but those who hope in the Lord will renew their strength. They will soar on wings like eagles; they will run and not grow weary, they will walk and not be faint" (NIV).

Have you ever seen an eagle soar? That majestic bird does not beat frantically with his wings in order to get airborne. He waits perched on some rock until he feels an updraft of air, then spreads his wings to soar on that current so that he doesn't wear himself out fanning the air. Perhaps we should take a cue from that eagle. Life takes us through various phases. Sometimes we find ourselves soaring in productive activity while at other times we find ourselves fatigued and needing to settle down and rest. Again we wait, but always expecting God to surprise us with the next updraft of his Spirit. Who knows when and where and how it will come? But that it will come and that he will breathe out again the breath of his Spirit, I have no doubt—and maybe—if he has yet another surprise in store—that will include meeting you—my father and mother—in this life or the next!